WORKING WOMEN AND CHILD DEVELOPMENT

A SOCIOLOGICAL STUDY

Working Women and Child Development

A SOCIOLOGICAL STUDY

Sham Sun Nisa

ANMOL PUBLICATIONS PVT. LTD.
NEW DELHI - 110 002 (INDIA)

ANMOL PUBLICATIONS PVT. LTD.
Regd. Office: 4360/4, Ansari Road, Daryaganj,
New Delhi-110 002 (India)
Ph.: 23278000, 23261597
Branch Office: No. 1015, Ist Main Road, BSK IIIrd Stage
IIIrd Phase, IIIrd Block,
Bangalore - 560 085 (India)
Visit us at: www.anmolpublications.com

Working Women and Child Development: A Sociological Study

First Edition, 2009

ISBN 978-81-261-4105-0

PRINTED IN INDIA

Printed at Balaji Offset, Delhi.

CONTENTS

Acknowledgement *vii*

Preface *ix*

List of Tables *xiii*

List of Figures *xvii*

1. Working Women and Child Development: An Introduction 1
   - Women and Work
   - Determinants of Women's Work
   - Child Development
   - Women's Role–as a Mother
   - Working Women and Child Development
   - Working Women in Kashmir
2. Review of Literature 21
3. Methodology 34
4. Findings of the Study 44
5. Conclusion 90

Bibliography 105

Appendices: Interview Schedule 113

Index 122

ACKNOWLEDGEMENT

All thanks to Almighty Allah, the most Beneficent and Merciful, who gave me courage to complete this work. Here I feel bound to mention the role of various personalities who have contributed to the completion of this work. First of all I would like to express my sincere feelings and gratitude to my guide & mentor, Dr. Aneesa Shafi, Head of the Department of Sociology and Social Work, University of Kashmir, without whose able guidance, valuable suggestions and affectionate encouragement I would have wandered aimlessly in an endless labyrinth.

I feel highly obliged to Prof. Bashir Ahmad Dabla, who provided me with the broad frame work and general guidance within which I carried out my work and for the valuable help he has rendered to me.

I can't forget the invaluable help which the staff members and particularly the Librarian of this Department and the Library staff of the *Iqbal Library* for providing me the literature I needed from time to time.

I am also thankful to the H.O.D. Psychology and the staff members of that Department for their cooperation.

I am as ever beholden to my family members and I wish to express my sincere thanks to my parents, who have always been a source of inspiration and encouragement to me from the very inception of my career. Their encouragement and good wishes have played a major role in the completion of this work. I again thank them for providing me material support throughout the course of my study.

I would be failing in my duty if I didn't acknowledge the support of my elder brother *Mr. Mubashir Hassan,* for the immense help at the various stages of the study which he always rendered to me. It would be doing injustice to my sisters if I don't mention their role which they played by performing each and every domestic work and leaving me free for these pursuits. Besides, the support of my grand mother and cousins can't be overlooked.

I also thank everyone who has helped me either directly or indirectly in completion of this study.

Last, I thank all the respondents without whose cooperation the present study wouldn't have been a possibility.

Sham Sun Nisa

PREFACE

Kashmiri society is known for its simplicity and for its unique tradition. Kashmir valley is not easily connected with the rest of the world, so the technology and the cultural impact of the outside world did not make its foray into the valley for until recently. As a consequence people remained confined to their own culture and the past tradition continued through generations. Any sway from its culture and tradition was bitterly resented and as such change was never welcome.

In the traditional Kashmiri society, the male members would work in the agricultural fields, in their orchards or would engage in any other gainful employment like paper machine, chain stitching, carpet weaving etc. and the women would stay at home. They too would engage in household chores and sometimes also took to some gainful work like carpet weaving etc. But remained confined to their homes. Looking after children was the responsibility of mother and other women folk of the family and as there were many women in the household, looking after children was an easy job. At bed time, the children would be told stories ....horror stories, of brave heroes, of Jinns and of the cruelties of life. They shared their thoughts. The personality of elders penetrated into that of the child's and he would mature with these instincts, mingled with traditional and cultural traits.

However, it was not to continue indefinitely. It had to change and it did change. Women came out of their homes and began to work along with men. Initially some women hesitated to come out of their homes, but slowly the number of women coming out of their homes went on increasing. Slowly the education level among women also rose and more and more women sought to work outside their homes.

There was also a change in the out look of people. People began to seek earning women as daughter's-in-laws and/or as wives. As the economies of those who had working women as their wives or daughter-in-laws improved largely, the trend changed. There was a high demand for working women and those women who did not work/earn were not much sought in marriages. The result was late marriages. The girls began to get high education so as to get employment. Marriages were postponed and emphasis was on gainful employment. It was during this period that electronic Media too made its entry into this secluded valley and their was an impact of western culture in the valley. Privatization of the Insurance Companies, banks and finance companies had its own impact: Many jobs were made available to youth and girls were particularly encouraged by these companies to join.

There was a complete overhaul of the society. The traditional and cultural values were lost. The role of family changed completely. There were new aspirations, new goals, new themes and new aims. All this happened because woman broke the traditional roles and came out of her home.

The worst sufferer of all this was the child. There was no one to look after him. He was left alone to make his way in this world. The love and affection which a child was showered with in the traditional Kashmir society were lost. Today's child appears to be lonely without any support. He has to care for himself. He is alone. He suffers silently, he weeps silently. He has no one to confide in. In foreign societies, the people have developed means to take care of their children, but all these facilities/experiences are lacking in Kashmir. This book would prove to be an eye opener and would help in realization of this neglected problem. And would make people realize that economy is not everything.

LIST OF TABLES

3.1	Age, sex and type of school (Sampling plan)	39
3.2	Nature of the family. (Sampling plan)	39
3.3	Mothers' occupation. (Sampling plan)	40
4.1	Care of children during office time.	46
4.2	Satisfaction of mother to the day care arrangement.	47
4.3	Reasons for being satisfied with the day care arrangement	47
4.4	Reasons for not being satisfied with the day care arrangement	48
4.5	Time leaving for office	48
4.6	Preparation for leaving for the office	49
4.7	Time spends with the children	49
4.8	Reasons for not spending sufficient time with the children	50
4.9	Respondents satisfaction for spending time with the children	50
4.10	Dietary behavior of children	52
4.11	Feeding of children before the proper time	52
4.12	Mothers' satisfaction towards the children's feeding	53
4.13	Improper feeding affects the health of these children	53
4.14	Improper feeding affects the psyche of these children	54
4.15	Breast feeding of children	56
4.16	Satisfaction of mother to the breast-feeding of the children	57

4.17 Reasons for not been able to breast-feed their children 57

4.18 Mothers need during the day 59

4.19 Reasons behind the mothers need during the day 60

4.20 Attention to the child after returning from the office 61

4.21 Reasons for inattention towards the children 61

4.22 Care of sick children 62

4.23 Respondents satisfied to the performance of mothering role 63

4.24 Mothers' absence creates problems during the day 64

4.25 Type of problems created by the absence of the mother 65

4.26 Preparation for the school 68

4.27 Educational Guidance outside school 69

4.28 Mothers' presence in the school function 70

4.29 Respondents' attitude towards the mother's absence in school functioning 71

4.30 After returning from school mother's presence 72

4.31 Respondents' feeling on finding her mother at home after school 72

4.32 Respondents' feeling on not finding her mother at home after school 73

4.33 Respondents' activity on holidays 74

4.34 Feeding of the children in absence of the mother 75

4.35 Respondents' satisfaction/dissatisfaction on being fed by other agencies 75

4.36 Comparison of respondents' on being fed by her mother or by other agencies 76

4.37 Care of children during illness 77

4.38 Mothers' going to office or staying at home during the child's illness 78

4.39 Need of mother during illness 78

4.40 Reasons for need of mothers' presence during illness 79

4.41	Child care during mothers' absence	80
4.42	Respondents' feelings towards the other agencies looking after them in absence on their mothers	81
4.43	Activity of working women after returning from office (as revealed by their children	82
2.44	Mothers' appearance after returning from office	83
4.45	Time spends by working women spend outside home (as revealed by their children)	84
4.46	Activities performed by working women on holidays	85
4.47	Outings with mothers'	86
4.48	Grievance of children against mothers' job	86
4.49	Mothers' attitude towards respondent's misbehaviour	88
4.50	The agencies guiding children in their behaviour	88

LIST OF FIGURES

3.1	Nature of the Family	40
4.1	Respondents satisfaction for spending time with children	51
4.2	Mothers need during the day	59
4.3	Respondents satisfied to the performance of mothering role	63
4.4	Child care during mothers' absence	81

1

WORKING WOMEN AND CHILD DEVELOPMENT: AN INTRODUCTION

In today's world pursuing a specific occupation, the virtues of hard work, frugality, responsibility, steady work habits, are all greatly valued. The need for security and recognition becomes closely associated with getting and keeping the job. The high prestige value of a good position (in terms of job), especially that which provides a handsome remuneration, leads to rising aspirations which may result in a better quality of life. Thus work becomes an integral part of life both for men as well as for women. However, there is a strong belief that a woman's place is in the home with her children because of the societal norms. Once under the surface of the issue; however, there is much more to be considered than just whether to stay home with her children or not. There are many variables of the issues pressing on a mother in today's society. Economic, social and emotional issues combine to make a mother's choice, whether to stay at home with her children or work outside the home, the hardest decision many women ever face.

Many women work simply because changes in the economy have made it necessary for many married women to work. Living costs, such as housing and food prices, have risen. Thus, for most married couples or two parent families it is necessary to have two incomes to maintain the standard of living it was once possible to attain with a single wage-earner.

For many married women, the income from the husband alone is not enough to support the family, thus there is a need, not just a want, for the mother to work and ease some of the financial burdens of the family. Many families can not feed those babies unless mothers outside work. Many researchers believe that as the cost of living continues to rise, many more families will be forced to have both parents work outside homes.

Women and Work

As far as "women and work" is concerned there has been a significant increase in women's participation in the work force not withstanding their contribution at the home front. This is more significant in view of generally held view that whether it is professional field or home or anywhere, efficiency of women is comparatively higher than their male counterparts.[1]

Looking back, women have primarily been associated with the home and men with the world of work. As home makers, women are expected to look after the domestic front. This involvement however, varies in different socio-economic conditions and in different regions. Thus women, irrespective of their involvement in economic activities of any kind, are expected to be home makers along with efficient workers in the work situation. Most women understand their role and do have a forward looking ambition. They are satisfied if men understand there aspirations ignoring traditional and conservative attitude regarding involvement of women in gainful employment. Women in the context of development—cultural, social, political, economic and psychological—have been restrained in their quest for selfhood and autonomy. It is only recently that they have started coming out of their seclusions and are marching ahead in the world of work.[2]

The women's movement– also variously called the feminist movement, women's liberation movement or women's rights movement– is a transformational social movement that focuses on changing the mostly institutional and social attitudes, beliefs, activities, practices and identities that form the basis of social life arranged according to an assumed gender hierarchy. It was the Industrial Revolution; with its wide spread social changes which caused the women's movement to develop rapidly. It opened women's eyes to the fact that their economic dependence on men and their lack of educational, political and social opportunities were key factors in their subordinate position in society. Throughout the nineteenth century women worked together to address needs and grievances; by the first half of the twentieth century they had won the right to vote, control their earnings, own property and be employed. The women's movement in the second half of the twentieth century sought to took the lead in fighting for total emancipation.

There are evidences to show that the traditional view regarding the place and role of women is slowly loosing ground in contemporary society. The process has been generated and aided by a variety of factors which are operating simultaneously. Increasing opportunities for modern education, greater geographical and occupational mobility, and the emergence of new economic patterns may be cited as a few possible factors for such a change.

This however should not be viewed as replacement of tradition by modernity; rather it should be treated as modernized tradition, failing which it would lead to "modernity" becoming rootless and deficient. The ongoing movements on women's upliftment should thus focus on women's development in every respect by not destroying the very basis of women's structure. That is to say that 'women should join work force' is emphasised, but by not letting their role in the home front pushed in a relegated position.

This means that women will have to try to combine career with social institution. For the single women, however, a career outside the home may well afford her an integrating centre for her life. But that of a women who has to or wishes to combine 'gainful' employment with the duties and pleasures of wife and others—can she effectively combine the two? It has been argued that, when a women enters into 'gainful employment' she has to perform dual functions—one in the home (feminine role) and other outside the home (gainful employment).[3] Thus, for a married working woman there are three significantly different roles to be played simultaneously—the roles of a wife, a mother and a worker leading to the possibility of role conflict.

The motives to seek employment and the resulting role conflict are closely related. The women who are simply interested to do a job or who thought that it would give them a sense of economic independence, did not perceive their employment interfering with child care attendants, on the other hand those who did not have any inner urge but rather forced by circumstances did perceive that their outside work interfered with child care responsibilities.[4]

The most common problem faced in entering the work force is household responsibilities. Incapacity to hire household help, traditional time consuming food habits and the scarcity of child-care centers are the factors which increase the burden of household responsibility. Lack of enough capital is another significant constraint.

Determinants of Women's Work

Educated women take up jobs or professions not only out of sheer economic necessity but also out of various other socio-psychological-situational reasons.

The causes that prompt women to enter into employment are as complex as those influencing other choices that affect their way of life. It is generally believed that socio-cultural changes play a significant role in creating a situation in which women would like to seek employment. While one would not deny the importance of socio-cultural changes, there are several other factors which lead one to take individual decision to work or not to work. It might be that in a particular cultural context, woman was in a position to get employment but her desire might not be translated into action if she was not in a position to get out of home.

In one of the ILO studies dealing with women's employment it was presumed that motives differed with marital status both objectively and subjectively. Not only the economic needs but the motivational reasons also vary with marital status. They broadly mentioned two reasons. (a) Women's economic need and (b) national necessity for increased production.[5]

Zweing, F. has discussed that the loneliness is a powerful motive for women to seek employment outside their homes.[6] In *International India,* a Publication of *Ministry of Labour and employment,* Government of India, it has been pointed out that whatsoever the stage of economic or social development of a country, four factors prevail which lead women to join work force. They are: (a) inadequate income of the principal earner which forces a woman to work and supplement the income (b) mishap, such as incapacity of the bread winner (c) death of the bread-winner, and (d) a women's desire for economic independence or for securing higher standard of living. There is also the desire on the part of the women to give expression to their own talents and skills.[7]

Apparently money is not the sole motive for their being in jobs. This has been evinced by the fact that there are women who are in jobs mainly out of their love for profession or career and after getting married, when their financial worries had vanished, they didn't give up their work but remained enthusiastic as earlier. They have a desire to maintain their individual interests and status; and want to pursue their jobs in order to satisfy their intellectual need and quest for recognition and fame. It is interesting to note that there are working women who, even though not ambitious or attached to their professions or jobs as such, continue to be in jobs even after marriage because they are "used to working". An idea of the working women after getting "used to working"—outside involvement, particular routine, individual status and independent income—they can not reconcile to the idea of sitting at home only as housewives. And so they continue to be in jobs even when it is no longer an economic necessity. That money is not the exclusive motive for married women's employment, is also indicated by the fact that even wives, whose husbands have a reasonably high income, are in jobs.[8]

Child Development

The mother is the first to socialize the child. She is not only closely related to the child but physically she is nearest to him than others. From the mother/parents the child learns his speech and language. He is taught societal morality. The family is rightly called the cradle of virtues. The child gets his first lessons in cooperation, tolerance, self sacrifice, love and affection from his mother.[9]

However, the meaning of the mother–child relationship can only be understood properly if observed from the child's point of view. How the child sees the situation may or may not be in line with what the mother/parents have in mind. Although mother's/parents behaviour is an objective event in the real world, it affects the child's ego development only to the extent and in the form in which he perceives it. Hence perceived behaviour is in reality a more direct, relevant and proximate determinant of personal development than the actual stimulus context to which it refers".[10]

Although there is multiplicity of theories on this aspect, only a few of these which emphasize parental influence on the child's developmental process are described below:

1. Psychoanalytic Theory: The psychoanalytic theory was propounded by Freud. Being a psychoanalyst, he interpreted every action in terms of psychoanalysis. According to this theory personality development is a succession of stages and each stage characterized by a dominant mode of achieving libidinal pleasure. The stages are: Oral, Anal, Phallic, Latency and Genital. Freud believed that gratification during infancy may become prone to excessive eating or drinking and develop such "character traits" as greediness, high dependency and passivity. He emphasized on the effect of early childhood experiences in latter personality adjustment. According to Freud many events that have occurred in childhood are significant enough to create an impression, (positively or negatively) will influence the development in later life. For instance, we might consider a child whose achievements were never recognized or encouraged, will feel shy in sharing his feelings related to achievement in severe cases he may loose interest and tend to become the "withdrawal" type.

2. The Behaviouristic Approach: The behaviouristic school of thought attempts to explain the acquisition, modification and extinguishing of all types of behaviours. Maladaptive behaviour is essentially viewed as the result of

(a) a failure to learn necessary adaptive behaviours or competencies, such as how to establish satisfying personal relationship.

(b) Learning ineffective or maladaptive responses, e.g. how an irrational fear or 'phobia' could be reality learned through conditioning.

(c) Stress situations that the individual feels incapable of dealing with.

This school of thought elaborately talks of "Generalization" and "Discrimination" which occurs as a result of conditioning. Behaviourists emphasize that processes like understanding, attitude forming, perceiving, solving, concept learning etc, are all an outcome of learnt tendencies of generalization and discrimination. Since family is the most immediate and important learning situation, it becomes the duty of family members to help in forming positive 'generalization' and 'discrimination'.

3. The Humanistic Thought: This model was advocated by William James, Gorden Allport, Abraham Maslow, Carl Rogers, Fritz Pearls. Here they emphasize on development of self, values and personal growth. They take a positive view of human nature and potential for which family indeed plays a significant role. According to this model, psychopathology is essentially the blocking or distortion of personal growth. This is generally the result of either the exaggerated use of ego defence mechanism so that the individual becomes increasingly out of touch with reality or, unfavourable social conditions and faulty learning, or excessive stress.

Rogers particularly talks of self and development of self. If the self is not rightly valued or self development is hampered the result is distortion in behaviour patterns. Humanistic psychologists lay stress on individuality, (individuality) as a consequential effect of genetic inheritance and social environment. Maslow (1969) has pointed out it is essential that we develop a "good society" as well as a" good person" It is the primary role of the family to put the child in favourable conditions.

4. Existentialists View: A basic theme of existentialism is that our existence is given (how the child is brought up). Family has a major share of responsibility regarding this. The model further emphasizes on Choice, Freedom and Courage. Morris (1966) has stated the situation in the form of three propositions (a) I am a choosing agent- unable to avoid choosing my way through life. (b) I am a free agent- absolutely free to set the goals of my own life. (c) I am a responsible agent, personally accountable for my free choices as they are revealed in how I live my life. How and what the individual chooses, how independent is he and how responsible he is- depends largely on the family he belongs to. And it is the family that should moulds the inner self of a child.

Underlying these three agents is the "courage". The strength to choose the type (of self) is to set the goals independently without any bias or influence to feel responsible enough to take the right decision. Now, whether the child has developed the courage in him is a direct consequence of familial influence on him. It is the courage to live that is to be developed, which would result in positive feeling towards oneself and develop the strength to live on. These things would be developed only in a proper family environment.

5. The Interpersonal Model: The interpersonal model emphasis on unsatisfactory interpersonal relationships as the primary cause for many forms of maladaptive behaviours. Such relationships may extend back to childhood and later socialization period, where the child is influenced by significant others.

According to Sullivan One's personality development proceeds through various stages involving different patterns of interpersonal relationships. The first interaction is mainly with parents, who begin the socialization of the child. Later, with adolescence and a gradual reluctance from parents and greater inclination towards peer relationships and in young adulthood intimate relationships are established. Failure to progress satisfactorily through these stages of development becomes a cause for later maladaptive behaviours. He further stresses on the role of family and parent in shaping the self-concept of the child which he perceives as developing largely out of the reflected appraisal of the significant others, where family comes first. Continual appraisal by others lead the child to brand himself as "good me" or "bad me". The "good me" gives him a pleasant feeling and the "bad me" is associated with anxiety. If this anxiety producing situation becomes too intolerable, the child learns to perceive himself as "not me", which is definitely a distorting, disorienting factor for personality development.

Women's Role–as a Mother

Women, as a social category, perform multiple roles. Certain types of roles have been universally recognised and socially institutionalized. The biological woman is the product of nature, but the socio-cultural woman is structurally created and conditioned. The physical differentiation between man and woman necessitates certain social arrangements for procreation and rearing of children. A human child needs prolonged care during infancy, in contrast tc the animal. Only women can bear a child, but men can certainly rear it. The physical force of man makes him different from woman, but not superior. By her very nature, woman is tied to motherhood in a familial - social responsibility. Glorification of motherhood was a manipulative device to confine her to drudgery.

As soon as a woman attains the status of 'mother', she entails additional responsibility. A woman, as a mother, has a unique place in our society. Out of the two parents, the mother's role is greater and more significant. Being a mother she is the socializer of the new generation. Mother's interest and involvement in child gives a new status to her. She is the preserver of the 'cultural traditions' and socializer of young generation, and inculcates traditional values and norms to the young generation. These are her cultural roles and apart from these, she also plays a role in the development of the emotional psychology of the child.[11]

"Love of mother is an instrument of terrible potentiality. Because of its use we can so easily cow individuals into a semblance of proper conduct, we use it recklessly. We go further and extol the man who shows great devotion to his mother and to the man who can weep out at the name of "mother" we ascribe special virtue. The love of mother is too vulnerable an asset in the life of any man to run the risk of turning it into a liability through reckless use".[12]

Home environment, though a contributory effort of both—the mother and the father, later added by the efforts of children, a major share of it results from the contribution of the mother. Mother is understood to be a prime factor in the development of the child, as she spends most of her time satisfying the physical, mental and moral needs of the child. The influence of the mother on her child is particularly important. Mother's influence may lay the foundation of a happy and prosperous life or it may turn it towards disaster. It is from the mother specially that the child receives his first and lasting lessons of citizens. Mother is the most important socializing agent. The child receives from his mother valuable training of discipline and self-control.

In the study of individual-group interaction, the mother is the first and foremost in its influence. It is the mother to whom the child has his first social relationships in which and through which he acquires and organizes his experiences. No other institution has so significant a role in the transition of individual to a person as is of the mother's. In the first year of life, it is the mother's lap from which a child's "humanizing" process begins. Mother is said to be "the eternal school of social virtues" [13]. The mother is the first social agency from which a child holds a membership. She is also the first to teach him how to live with other people.

Working Women and Child Development

The substantial increase in the women's employment over the past has significantly affected the socio—psychological and family processes having a bearing on the children in home as it is the married women who face the challenges and problems in employment sector. For employed women there may be a number of reasons underlying the need to work, but the effect of mothers' employment on the well—being of their children does evoke special interest. When a woman takes up a job outside her home, she has to function as a wife, a mother and as a worker. This places additional responsibility on her requiring the skill, as well as capabilities of acceptance and adjustment to the change brought about by the multiplicity of roles. Out-of-home work by mothers' was analytically important for establishing whether, it did or didn't negatively influence the normative patterns of family life.

Women's employment is associated with numerous outcomes of interest and the effect of mothers entering into job market on the well-being of children evoked significant interest. Because of working women's continuing role of child rearing and home management, her entering into job life has affected home-front. There follows a remarkable change in family structure and family environment.[14]

Today more mothers work outside the home than before. How this affects children depends partly upon the provisions made for their care. It is assumed that the child usually feels lonely and unhappy when the mother is away for a major part of the day.[15]

In families where mother works, there is a greater possibility that the home duties will get neglected or postponed or transferred and there are fewer opportunities for social life and recreation with the family. Children of such families are more expected to share in the household activities as compared to children of non-working mothers. This also depended on the working ability of the mother.

Children of working mothers have been found to be less adjusted than children of non-working mothers. These children tend to be nervous and irregular in their work habits which affect their school adjustment.[16] It has been observed that young children are more affected by the mother's employment than older children.[17]

The mother's reason for working and her attitude towards work has a significant bearing on her role as a mother. Because employment doesn't fit into the cultural stereotype of "mother"; she may feel guilty about being away from home, especially if working is not motivated by economic necessity.[18]

The newborn infant comes into the world with no inherited predispositions, but rather with a mind as a "blank slate" that is gradually filled with ideas, concepts, and knowledge from experiences in the world. The early experiences, particularly how children are raised and educated, shapes the direction of a child's life. This statement is sufficient to realise the importance of guidance and socialization for a child. And who can be a better socializer and a better guide than a mother?

Many social psychologists, William McDougall, John B. Watson, E.A. Ross, Floyd Allport, introduced the concept of attachment. They proposed that infants and young children form emotional bonds to their care-givers because, throughout human evolutionary history, close attachments to mother promoted the survival of defenseless children.

Attachment is a psychological bond between an infant and her or his primary care giver, i.e. the mother. Crying and smiling bring infants in contact with care givers and are called attachment behaviours. Attachment provides a secure emotional base from which mature relationship develops. Research shows that inadequate attachment impedes social and emotional development throughout life. For example, when an infant is subjected to maternal deprivation, and thus does not form a secure attachment, subsequent development is often severely atypical. Mother is always the first and foremost in children's lives. That's absolutely essential to children who need good quality care in their families.[19]

Researchers have shown that an infant can't develop physically as well as mentally, if he is not receiving the message of attachment and love. It is well known that no one can take care of a child as a mother can. The first agent of socialization is the mother for a child. It is saying that 'the family revolves round the child and the child revolves round the mother'. PHIL PONCE rightly said that "the good quality or the best quality child care centers do not provide what a mother provides".[20]

Child rearing has posed the biggest challenge to the working mothers. The problem starts with pre-school care when the mother leaves the infant with a relative or a maid, or puts him/her in a crèche. Due to the change in the joint family system to the nuclear family system, elderly family members, or aunts and uncles, along with the elderly cousins are no longer at hand to look after the children. The maids being unreliable and difficult to procure, apart from being expensive, the only alternative remains the crèches or day care centers.

Unlike in the good old joint families, the absence of elderly presence in the modern nuclear families leaves the working mother with no option but to leave the child in a day care centers. Here comes the role of a crèche or play school to substitute the tender care of home for a blooming child much to the relief of young working mothers. [21]

Some mothers are hiring the services of servants to look after their children. Baby sitters are usually paid to watch, play with and care for the children. But the purpose would be served only if the children received their sitters' full attention.

Care and love are synonyms for what mothers have given their children since the beginning of time. Child-care has become a major issue in contemporary times, making us realise that our children are in need of love. The optimum situation is a family member whom can provide day-care, but this is not always an option.

What does a child want to do after coming back from school? Surely he or she would yearn for the caressing arms of his or her mother. This scarcely is the tendency nowadays as a majority of mothers are working outside their homes leaving their children at the mercy of various unnatural institutions. Merely paying the fee and dressing up the child are not enough but the involvement of a parent is more important for a child's mental and physical growth.[22]

Children who receive attention from their parents develop properly, physically as well as mentally. If children get attention when they are young, they are able to cope better as teenagers. Children who have a close bond with their parents are more apt to talk to parents. A mother spends time with the child but that time must be quality time (quality time here means give the child the feeling that you are thinking about him only).[23] The attention a child receives during early years is irreplaceable. The amount of attention a child receives influences his or her direction in life.[24]

Working Women in Kashmir

In past the lives of the people were simple. The economy was agrarian. People lived simple lives and religion held sway over their lives. It was generally believed that the ideal place for a woman from birth till death is the family household. Consequently, they were confined to their homes throughout their lives and were hardly exposed to outside world. Women were also supposed to be completely dependent on their men, fathers and husbands or brothers. Men used to earn and spend their money while women worked within the family household. In traditional society, women's role was limited to the family. Since she was the bearer of the children, she was fully occupied with her role as a mother and home maker.

In traditional times women spend most of their time with their children. They were with them (Children) when they need their mothers. During infancy period children need their mothers. In past mother was present at the time when the child needs her; during stress and strain the children has some one to rely upon. He/she found himself/herself in the loving care of his/her mother. Whenever such children faced some upheavals in life, their mother was there for support and to share their burden. Naturally the life of such children was free from emotional upheavals and rarely suffered psychic problems.

The condition of women in Kashmir started undergoing change in the early decades of twentieth century according to experts. Factors like emerging political consciousness, improvement in the means of transportation and communication, spread of formal education and socio—cultural awakening created an environment in which women tried to access their position in the society. Thus, in the changing scenario women belonging to all classes, groups and communities started coming out of their homes for the attainment of formal education and even taking up careers in different governmental and non governmental organizations. Their participation is also found in social fields, welfare activities administrative services and other bureaucratic jobs. They are contesting elections and participating in the deliberations of state legislatures. In short they have made their presence in every field of life.

This, in turn, creates problems for the 'family organization' which is the basic institution of the society. For Kashmiri women these substantial changes have given new challenging roles. Apart from the motherhood and domestic work, they have to undertake an active role in economic organization. Because of outside as well as domestic work they have not as much of time to spend with their children, this affects the family organization badly. They (working women) have less time to look after their children, to attend to their needs; to chastise them when they go wrong.

The present study investigates the nature of the problems of children whose mothers' are working outside their homes and to analyze their day care arrangements, nutritional, health and psychological problems. Furthermore it is intended to examine the impact of the mothers' employment on the socialization process of these children.

It is necessary to consider the expectations which the society places upon the behaviour of each sex in general as well as differential role in the child training; which is expected of men and women in particular. Considering the latter expectations first, it would seem that the mother is held more responsible than is the father for the home affairs, particularly caring for the children.

REFERENCES

1. Sircar Basobi, "Working Mothers and Adolescent Wellbeing" Commonwealth Publishers, New Delhi, 1994.
2. Singh, K.P., "Career and Family—Women: Two Roles", *Indian Journal of Social Work,* 1972.
3. *Ibid.*
4. *Ibid.*
5. Myrdal, Alva and Viola Klein, "Women's Two Roles", London Routledge and Kegan Paul, 1962. (An International Survey of the conditions of Working Women with Home and Family Responsibilities)
6. Zweing, F. "Women's Life and Labour", London: Victor Gallanz, 1952.
7. Government of India, "International India," Women in Employment, Labour Bureau, Ministry of Labour and Employment, 1964.
8. *Op. cit.* Sircar Basobi.
9. Hurlock, E.B., "Child Growth and Development", fourth edition. McGraw Company, 1950.
10. Johnson, M. Harry, "Sociology, Themes and Perspectives", Rawat Publications, New Delhi, 1989.
11. Menaghan, E.G., & Parcel, T.L. "Parental Employment and Family Life: Research in the 1980s." *Journal of Marriage and the Family,* 1990.
12. Frank Wood, E. "Psychology of Adolescence", London: Rutledge and Kegan Paul, 1948.
13. *Op. cit.,* Basobi Sircar.
14. Nye and Hoffman, L.W., "The Employed Women in America" Rand McNally and company, Chicago, 1963.
15. Coleman, J.C., "Abnormal psychology and Modern life" 5th edition, Scott, Foreman and Company, 1976.

16. Hurlock, E.B., "Child Growth and Development". Mc Graw Hill Book Company Kogahusha Ltd.
17. Rouman, J., "School children's problems as related to presented factors". *J. Educational Research,* 1956.
18. *Op. cit.,* E.B. Hurlock.
19. Sinha, Pupsa, "Role conflict among working women" Janaki Prakashan Publishers, New Delhi, 1988.
20. Ponce, Phil, " A Real Mother in the Modern World". A report on child care on brain development leads to a call for better child care. January 22, 1997.
21. Luecken, Linda, "A Duke University study on stress in working moms" Veteran of the department of psychiatry at Duke University Medical Center in Durham.
22. *Op. cit.,* Basobi Sircar
23. *Ibid.*
24. Kontos, S.J., "Child Care Quality, Family Background, and Children's Development." *Early Childhood Research Quarterly,* 1991.

2
REVIEW OF LITERATURE

In the pages to follow, an attempt has been made to briefly present a 'Review of Literature' available on the issues and problems surrounding working women and their children.

Rani[1] in a study of "Performance of Job Role by Working Women" found that industrialization had brought about a continuing shift from family centered to factory centered production. She categorized working women as those to whom employment gave an opportunity to use their individual talents and educational qualifications and those who were least likely to experience major conflicts in their responsibilities towards their children and to receive negative reactions from their husbands and relatives. The work atmosphere, working hours, length of service, performance on the job and commitment to the job were mainly considered and it was found that the performance of job role dependent upon the working conditions. The conditions of work depended upon the profession of the respondent. Analysis showed that profession, education or income did not have a bearing on the performance of the job role. A very large number of respondents felt that their jobs were interesting and did not believe that marriage was an impediment in carrying out the job role.

Promilla Kapur[2] in her study, "Marriage and Working Women in India" analyzes socio- psychological aspects of working women of India. The study seeks to find out co-relation between mal-adjusted married life and employment of working women. The finding is that women's taking up job out-side the home does not adversely affect their marital life. Women gave more importance to their roles as wife and mother which helped to maintain their feminine virtues of tolerance, sacrifice and humility.

Promila Kapur's[3] second study "Changing Status of Working Women in India" is an empirical study of a broader context and aims at studying urban educated young working women. The study highlights the changing attitudes of working women towards their own status and role, towards society, family and children. She pointed out that women's taking up a job outside the home is more looked down upon. This change is perceptible. The author has also tried to identify the source of conflict between women's dual roles: the traditional role of house wife and mother and that of the worker who is gainfully engaged in employment outside the home. Their adjustment in the male-dominated employment milieu is also discussed, included in the study are instances of successful women in unusual occupations. The work highlights the manifold aspects concerning the working conditions, strains and stresses as well as prospects of working women in India.

Krishna Chakraborthy[4] in her article "The Conflicting Worlds of Working Mothers" tried to examine the role conflict of educated working mother. She studied and judged the impact of outside remunerative employment on working mothers themselves. She attempts to clarify the position of women in society. The study investigates the factors behind the role conflict. The occupational status and role conflict and role congruency was also measured in relation to the respondent's jobs. The study underlined the fact that working mothers underwent various types of role conflicts. These role conflicts differed widely and no single factor or a set of factors taken together can conclusively bring out the full import of a respondents role conflict experience.

Singh,[5] in her study "Career and Family Women's two Roles" (a study in role conflict), pointed out that only 25% of the working women were fully satisfied with the time they were devoting to their children. 70% felt that they really could not devote proper attention to their children and home as the major part of their day was spent outside the house.

The study revealed that among women who were working out of sheer economic necessity, the dissatisfaction prevailed among majority. The study concluded that the motivation employment and the role conflict are closely related.

Nye and Hoffman[6] in their study "The Employed Women in America" have pointed out that there were only a few changes which affected so many families in such a few years as the movement of mothers into paid employment had a greater impact on the family structure than on specific aspects of the children's psychological adjustment. By tradition the mother's place was in the home and she looked for outside work only if the family's economic situation so warranted. The position taken by particular group of psychologists that the child's eventual personality development depended upon a close relationship with his mother during his early years lent support to this point of view. This position stressed that unless there was continuous mother figure present, harmful consequences were likely to ensue.

It seems that mother's employment outside the home altered the family's traditional structure, including such aspects of family relationship like the managing of household work, decision making, dominance role etc. When the responses of children of working mothers were compared with those of non-working mothers, regarding parental performance of various household tasks, the former group reported that their mothers participated more in diverse areas. Related to this was the fact that working mothers made fewer decisions. However, with regard to general family decisions, especially in the economic area, the working wife played a more powerful role than the non-working one.

Tylor[7] conducted a study on "Role and Role Conflict in a Group of Middle—Class Wives and Mothers". The study found that the ideal role for all the wives and mothers expects them to place 'love and affection' high and maintenance of self low ideally speaking, the wife and mother see their role as self-sacrificing. The respondents of the study themselves thought that they see actually performing their role quite successfully. Such a self-perception was substantiated by the considerable absence of overall conflict.

Coleman, J.C.[8] in his study "Abnormal Psychology and Modern Life" had shown that families where both or either of the parents were not present, produce children with disturbances in their behaviour pattern, the degree of which varies to quite an extent. The disturbances may not always be easily observable. "By far the greatest number of infants subjected to maternal care". There the mother typically neglected the child, devoted little attention to him as was generally rejecting. The effect of such marked deprivation may be devastating.

Kuzma[9] in her study "Working Mothers" pointed out that mothers' should spend most of their time with their children. A child needs attention of his elders especially during the critical years of his/her age (infancy to adolescence). She adds that mothers have a life time to spend with their relatives, husbands, neighbours and friends, but a critical time to spend with their children is limited within the child's few short years when they are growing up in the home. She added that parents are the first teachers of children especially mother, and it is the responsibility of the mother to take care of their children. She further adds that during teen's children need attention of their elders, if they feel that elders do not give proper attention to them, they become frustrated and try to find that type of love some where else.

The study revealed that mothers should spend meaningful time with their children and give them emotional support, so that they can cope as better teenagers.

Sircar[10] in her study "Working Women and Adolescence Well-Being" pointed out, that no matter whatever may be the situation around children, their perception of situation is more important. Child's perception of the situation as positive or negative affects his behaviour more significantly than whether the situation is bad or good in its real sense. Here the author tries to show that in child hood thoughts come into being as a result of what goes on in the mind of the child. He (child) perceives the situation of his own. Child's early life experiences have marked influence on his later life. If he were to come across some difficulties during child hood and passes it over, it will be problematic for him for the future. She adds if the mother's working outside created tension in the family or other house-hold chores were affected and on top of that some responsibility shifted on the shoulders of children (particularly young children), they would resent mothers working.

The findings of the study shows that the stricter the home atmosphere;

(a) a more hatred relationship to parents
(b) more rejection of teachers
(c) poor relations with classmates
(d) more quarrels and shyness
(e) more worry, anxiety and guilt feeling
(f) more unhappiness and crying.
(g) More dependence on parents, but,
(h) better school grades and stronger ambition.

Smith, S. M, and A. J. Davis[11], in their study "Employed Mothers and Family Day –Care Substitute Caregivers" revealed that some working mothers keep the baby sitters to take care of their children. They spend less time with their children. They are around the children during the day time; as such they (working mothers) are not able to keep watch on their children whether they are wrong or right. The findings of the study show that these children have less morals and values on which to base their thinking or actions. They further added that lack of parental supervision is also the cause of educational problems now-a-days.

A study conducted by National Institute of Public Cooperation and child development (1978) revealed that (i) mothers employed as professionals were married to men who had handsome salaries, in many cases children had support of other members of the family and had effective mother substitutes during working hours, they also had help of domestic servants. Women employed in clerical and industrial jobs- unskilled and semi-skilled in urban and rural areas enjoyed comparatively less facilities. (ii) The results supported the expectations of a positive relationship between the existence of relevant service institutions in the area and the women's awareness of the institutional help for child care. (iii) The professionals had the highest remuneration and the shortest working day. The time, the mother spent in caretaking activities of the children under six years of age had direct relation to the type of her occupation. (iv) A favourable attitude of husbands towards their working wife reported by 84%, only 4% reported a negative attitude, 66% felt that the attitude of society towards working mothers was favourable. While 11% felt they had an unfavourable attitude, the findings were identical in both phases. (v) Most mothers in the upper occupational levels especially if they were educated, felt less dependent on the school for the child's social-development but wanted an institutional set-up of high quality for their children during working hours, the unskilled and semiskilled workers desired governmental institutions at no cost or at low cost, majority of the mothers interviewed felt the services were more acutely needed for children under three.

Aber and Bernreuter[12] reported in their study "Readings in Psychology of Parent-Child Relationship" of the personality traits of children in relation to their home discipline. Significant correlation appeared between physical punishment at home and a tendency of children to face reality, and between permissiveness of parents (letting children learn from the natural consequences of their acts) and a more "attractive" personality in the child.

Belsky and Hoffman[13], in their study "Effects of Early Parental Employment on Children" revealed that the past several decades have seen an increase in the number of employed mothers, with a particularly large increase in the frequency with which mothers of young children are employed. They were agreed that there is little evidence of negative effects when children are older. However, there remains debate about the effects of early maternal employment on children. Belsky and Hoffman concluded that maternal employment during infancy had ill effects on children's well-being. Specifically, they concluded that infants who were in non maternal care for more than 20 hr per week were at elevated risk for being insecurely attached at age 1 and were more disobedient and aggressive between ages 3 and 8.

Harry Harlow in her study[14] "Relationships Within the Family" revealed that parenting is such a complex area involving efforts to help and change children. There are many approaches to child-care, depending on the child's age and the problem. To produce happy, well adjusted, energetic, self-reliant, self-controlled, friendly, achieving children, (i) show children more love and genuine concern than hate, give more praise than criticism, and give more rewards than punishment. Spend time with them. (ii) Share your feelings and reasons with your children. Value their ideas; encourage verbal give and take. Touch them lovingly. (iii) Be fair, listen empathically and give respect, resolve differences by talking about problems as equals. (iv) Distinguish between the person and his/her actions. (v) Children need to be guided, corrected, and given high goals, values, responsibilities, and self-assigned chores, depending on the child's abilities and needs. They need help in becoming thoughtful of others. Encourage physical toughness and emotional strength; discourage dependency and demands for attention. (vi) Lastly, she wants to add a personal belief: every child deserves well trained parents, a child care specialist, and at least 2-4 hours a day away from parents. During this time away, the child should be with a skilled, experienced child care professional or teacher who also loves the child and collaborates or consults weekly with the parents. Raising a good human being should not be left to chance nor to untrained parents; child rearing takes more than a few minutes a day; it should be the highest priority.

D.W. Winnicott, in her study "Mirror-Role of Mother and Family in Child Development"[15] revealed that the proportion of working mothers with dependent children is increasing, especially among those with children under the age of five. Although the majority of mothers work part-time, increasing numbers are working full-time. Dramatic increases in mothers' employment are seen as having important effects on family life. Some argue that it makes mothers think of themselves as self-sufficient individuals rather than as someone who prioritizes their home life and family relationships. Others see it as leading to more equitable relationships between both partners in a couple, and to parents devoting quality time to their children.

The findings from this small-scale study do not wholly support either the negative or the positive perspective. This suggests that these theories tend to over-simplify working mothers' lives.

The researcher interviewed 37 mothers and 30 fathers in couples who had at least one pre-school child. The mothers were working in a hospital or in an accountancy firm. All the mothers in the study had strong, traditional views about what being a 'good mother' and a 'good partner' was about. Employment did not necessarily lead to more egalitarian relationships with their partners. She further added that most of the mothers and fathers, who were interviewed, subscribed to highly traditional and stereotypical views about the gendered division of labour within the home. The mothers had primary responsibility of the home and the conduct of family life. Mothers who worked full-time were just as concerned as those working part-time to 'be there' for their children and to meet the needs of their children and their family.

Abbott-Shim, M., and A. Sibley[16], in their study "Child Care Quality: Does it Matter and Does it Need to be Improved" revealed that Child care has become the norm for young children. This care typically began at early ages and lasted substantial hours. The use of non parental care is expected to grow even further as welfare reform is fully implemented. It is within this framework of widespread and early-age use that questions about child care quality have been raised. The child care established view is that child care quality contributes to children's developmental outcomes, higher quality care being associated with better developmental outcomes and poorer quality care being associated with poorer outcomes for children.

The findings of the study indicate that child care quality "matters" at several levels. In terms of children's everyday experiences, children appear happier and more cognitively engaged in settings in which caregivers are interacting with them positively and in settings in which child: adult ratios are lower. There also is evidence of concurrent relations between child care quality and children's performance in other settings. Children who attend higher-quality child care settings (measured by caregiver behaviours, by physical facilities, by age-appropriate activities, and by structural and caregiver characteristics) display better cognitive, language, and social competencies on standardized tests and according to parents, teachers, and observers. Finally, there is evidence that child care quality is related to children's subsequent competencies. The relationship is more evident when cumulative measures of child care quality are analyzed, rather than one-time assessments, and when quality and child care outcome measures have strong psychometric properties.

Elizabeth Harvey[17], in her study "Developmental Psychology" used a longitudinal design to examine the long-term effects of early parental employment-employment during the child's first three years of life—on the functioning of the child.

Dr. Harvey examined four employment variables: whether the mother worked during the first three years of the child's life, how soon a mother returned to work after child birth, how much she worked (hours per week) during the first three years of her child's life, and the discontinuity of employment (if there were any periods of unemployment during the same time frame). She compared these variables with five child outcome measures: compliance, behaviour problems, cognitive development, self-esteem and academic achievements.

Dr. Harvey found that children whose mothers worked during the first three years of their lives were not significantly different from children whose mothers did not work during that time frame. Among mothers who worked during the first three years of their child's life, the only significant effect of the timing of their return to work and the discontinuity of the employment was on compliance in three and four years olds. Three and four year old babies whose mothers returned to work later showed slightly higher compliance than the same age group whose mothers returned to work sooner, but these differences were small and disappointed by the time the children were five to six years of age. She also added that children whose mothers worked long were found to have slightly lower scores on tests, which measures children's vocabulary and individual student achievements, but again these differences were small and faded over time.

The studies above focus on the effects of women's work on their children. Some scholars have directly dwelled upon the problems suffered by the children whose mothers are working. While as some scholars have made indirect references; like the role conflict among women and the problems encountered by working women while bringing up their children and the consequences of it on their children. They also seek to examine the emotional and psychological aspects of the problems suffered by these children or in other words they have tried to examine how far the psyche of these children affected.

REFERENCES

1. Rani, K., "Performance of job role by working women", Indian Dissertation Abstract, 1936.
2. Kapur, Promila, "Marriage and the Working Women in India" Vikas Publishing House, New Delhi, 1970.
3. Kapur, Promila, "The Changing Status of Working Women in India" Vikas Publishing House, New Delhi, 1974.
4. Chakraborthy, Krishna, "The Conflicting Worlds of Working Mothers". *Sociological Inquiry*. Progressive Publishers, Kolkata, 1978.
5. Singh, K.P., "Career and Family—Women's Two Roles". *Indian Journal of Social Work*, Bombay, oct. 1972.

6. Nye and Hoffman, "The Employed Women in America". Dissertation Abstract Index, 1975, vol.29.
7. Tylor, P.H., "Role and Role Conflict in a Group of Middle-Class Wives and Mothers". *The Sociological Review,* New Series, vol. 12, No. 1, 1964.
8. Coleman, J.C. "Abnormal Psychology and Modern Life" 5th edition, Scott, Foreman and Company, Glenview Illinois, 1976.
9. K. Kuzma, "Working Mothers" Stratford Press, New York, 1981.
10. Sircar, Basobi, "Working Mothers and Adolescent Well-being". Commonwealth Publishers, New Delhi, 1994.
11. Smith, S. M., and A.J. Davis " Employed Mothers and Family Day-care Substitute Caregivers: A comparative analysis of infant care" child development 1984.
12. Aber, M.E. and R. Bernreuter, "Readings in Psychology of parent-Child Relationship" *Journal of Genetic Psychology,* 1977.
13. Belsky and Hoffman "Effects of Early Parental Employment on Children" a study conducted at Elizabeth Harvey University of Connecticut. 1999.
14. Harlow, Harry "Relationship within the family" Research Press, Champaign, 1984.
15. Winnicott, D.W. "Mirror-Role of Mother and Family in Child Development" In *Developmental Follow-Up: Concepts, Domains, and Methods,* ed. S. L. Friedman and H. C. Haywood. New York: Academic Press. 1992.
16. Abbott-Shim, M., and. Sibley, A, "Child Care Quality: Does it matter and does it need to be improved" Deborah Lowe Vandell and Barbara Wolfe Institute for Research on Poverty University of Wisconsin–Madison, 1992.
17. Harvey, Elizabeth, "Developmental psychology" New Longitudinal Study, University of Massachusetts at Amherst. 1999.

3
METHODOLOGY

PURPOSE AND METHODOLOGY

Recent years have brought a great change in the life of women all over the world, influencing their attitudes, values, inspirations, ways of feeling and acting for effective participation in all walks of life. One of the main enduring consequences of the recent social evolution for women has been their emancipation from their tradition bound ethos both legally and politically by the virtue of various acts and statuses. Now women have expanded the role of housewife into a dominant, mature feminine role.

Women's access to jobs may once have been a social issue, but in today's tough economic climate, working is now a necessity for most women. The bulk of families can no longer afford to live on one wage. Despite women's greater participation in the workforce, most men have yet to increase their share of domestic duties. This means that the majority of working mothers are also responsible for housework and looking after their children.

Women form an important part of the labour force and their role can't be isolated from the socio-economic development of the society. For the real progress of a nation it is significant that more and more women come out of their traditional roles and equally participate in the process of development of their respective societies. The changes that have taken place in the personality, attitudes and role of a woman, have had some crucial social implications. The main effects of the changes in women have shown upon the basic unit of the society i.e. Family.

The subject matter of the present study pertains to the impact of the work of the working women upon their children, particularly those who are below their teens and are being brought up. The impact is being investigated in the contemporary Kashmiri society which is facing different circumstances (because it lacks necessary infrastructure; besides the people are not mentally conditioned to the working-women-culture).

The children of working women, particularly those who are in the stage of being brought up, are affected by their work. Presumably a working woman may not find adequate time for her children, especially in a Kashmiri society (compared to the other parts of the globe); the substituting infrastructure is not adequately developed. Under such circumstances, the demands on working women are immense. And they often fail to meet the challenge, the consequences of which are borne by the children.

The present study aims to study the problems of the children of working women and the way they are affected by the work of their mothers.

The main concern of the present investigation is to find out the problems of the children whose mothers are working outside the home, their social, psychological and other related problems. The analysis of the existing literature on this subject and the studies conducted indicate diverse impacts on the children of working mothers. The present study concentrates on effects in the psyche, health, socialization and emotional stability of these children. Thus the present investigation aims at achieving the following objectives:

1. To evaluate the time constraint of the working women vis-à-vis day care arrangement for their children.
2. To examine the impact of the mothers' employment on the socialization process of these children.
3. To assess the nutritional problems of the children of working mothers.
4. To find out the health problems of the children of working mothers.
5. To analyze the psychological problems of the children of working mothers.
6. To evaluate possible remedies.

Hypothesis of the Study

In social research, each investigator is to start with certain assumptions and presumptions, which his subsequent study, might prove and disapprove. It is the hypothesis round which study revolves and for which data is collected. The hypothesis is a tentative justification, the validity of which remains to be tested.

In the light of the above objectives, it is intended to test the following hypothesis:

The hypothesis of this study is that the working women do not get sufficient time to spend with their children with the result their children suffer from various socio – psychological problems.

The Universe of the Study

The universe or the population is aggregate of all units, possessing certain specific characteristics of which the sample seeks to draw the conclusions. The universe of the study means the exact area where-from the individuals for the sample are selected. The universe for this study is the Srinagar City in the Srinagar District of the Kashmir valley.

Srinagar, which is the summer capital of the State Government, is named after its headquarters town like many other districts of the state. The boundaries of the Srinagar district extend from Baltal in the east to the mountain ranges about 16 km beyond Wangat in the north and to Toshmaidan in the south-west. It occupies the central sector of Kashmir valley and is intersected by the National Highways connecting Pathankot with Jammu, Srinagar and Ladakh.

The choice of Srinagar city as the universe of the study was made because Srinagar is the biggest commercial centre of J&K State and has the best possible cross-section of white collar and other office-based employees in the state.

Srinagar District is predominantly urban in character. According to the census of 2001, the total population of Srinagar is 118, 3493 in which males are 633,360 and females 550,133. The total literacy rate of the district is 59.31%. (Males: 68.99%; females: 48.11%). The breakdown of occupational structure by sex shows that 14.3% women are in the category of 'other services' which are dominant in white collar jobs (percentage of men is 85.7% are in the category of "other services").

Sample of the Study

The present study is carried out among the children of working women. The children who were selected for a

The below inset table gives the position of Srinagar District

Total Rural urban	Persons/ Males/ Females	Population 2001	1981	Growth of population 1981-2001	No. of workers 2001	1981	Increase/ Decrease in workers.	%age of col.8 to col.5
1	2	3	4	5	6	7	8	9
Total	persons	1,183,493	708,328	475,165	364,667	247,202	117,465	24.7
	Males	633,360	378,189	255,171	312,563	198,995	113,568	44.5
	Females	550,133	330,139	219,944	52,104	48,207	3,897	1. 8
Rural	Persons	253,357	138,133	115,224	76,666	72,274	4,392	3. 8
	Males	131,633	73,343	58,290	60,770	43,913	16,857	28.9
	Females	121,724	64,790	56,934	15,896	28,361	(-) 12,465	(-) 21. 9
Urban	Persons	930,136	570,195	359,941	288,001	174,928	113,073	31.4
	Males	501, 727	304,846	196, 881	251,793	155,082	96,711	49. 1
	Females	428,409	265,349	163, 060	36,208	19,846	16,362	10. 0

representative sample, was a conscious choice in order to give representation to the maximum number of children of working women. The whole sample comprised of 300 respondents. Out of these three hundred, 200 respondents were children from the age-group of 4-12 years and 100 respondents were those mothers whose children were below the age of 4 years and were not able to respond. Keeping in view the peculiar nature of the study it was decided to contact/consult their mothers to get responses.

As the universe was large and the sample to be selected small, the problem emerged with regard to the selection of actual sample units. Keeping in view the purpose of the study and broad characteristics of the universe, it was decided to choose 300 respondents from different age groups by random sampling.

3.1 Age, Sex and Type of School

Age Group	No. of children	sex Male	Female	Type of the school Private	Missionary Christian	Boarding	Govt.
4 months-4yrs	100	51	49	Not-school going			
4 6yrs	73	37	36	51	22	None	None
6–9yrs	83	41	42	65	18	None	None
9 – 12yrs	44	21	23	24	20	None	None
Total	300	150	150	140	60	0	0

3.2 Nature of the Family:

Age Group	No. of children	Nature of the Family Nuclear	Joint	Single parent
4 months-4 yrs	100	92	08	None
4–6yrs	73	63	08	02
6–9yrs	83	68	10	05
9 - 12yrs	44	36	05	03
Total	300	259	31	10

The study reveals that working mothers belong mostly (86.3%) to the nuclear families, besides 13.7% live in joint families or as single parents (either being widowed or divorced). Conjuring up the picture of these families, it would appear that the children of working women would face many difficulties as there would no body to look after them when their mothers are at work.

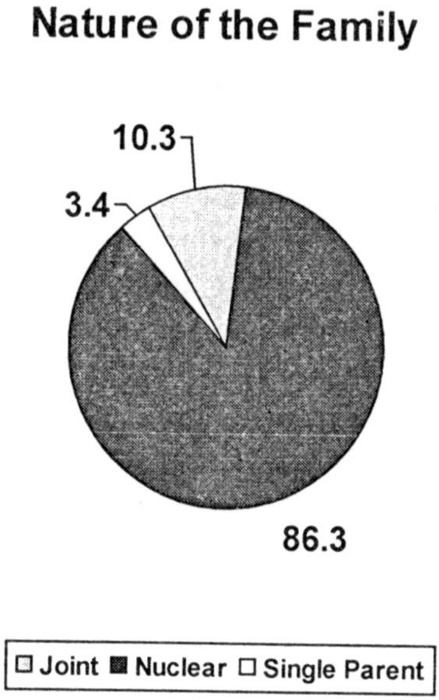

Fig 3.1

3.3: Mothers' occupation

Age Group	No. of children	Doctors	Lecturers	Teachers	Bank employees	Nurses	Other office workers
4 months-4 yrs	100	08	15	35	21	08	13
4 - 6yrs	73	04	10	20	13	09	17
6 - 9yrs	83	05	07	13	14	10	34
9-12yrs	44	03	04	12	10	08	07
Total	300	20	36	80	58	35	71

Tools and Techniques Used

After the selection of the sample the methods or techniques to be used by the researcher for the collection of the empirical data was selected. Under the peculiar circumstances, created by the type of research/respondents, the method of interview schedule seemed to be the best possible method.

In order to carry out a realistic research on the concerned topic, it was decided to elicit the information from the respondents through interview. The questionnaire method was ruled out as the researcher had to deal with children too little to respond satisfactorily to the questionnaire. A detailed and comprehensive interview schedule was prepared by the investigator to approach the respondents. In the interview schedule most of the questions were structured, listing alternative answers. The respondents had to choose the appropriate ones according to their own judgment, understanding and experience. Through interview one can get more information than other methods. Besides, while interviewing the respondents, the researcher made a keen observation of the respondents' actions and their conditions. However, the children who were below the age of 4 years were not able to respond, so it was decided to consult/contact their mothers in order to get information regarding the problems of children, in absence of their mothers.

For the collection of secondary data Books, Journals and Census reports were also consulted concerning the topic. The present study is mainly based on primary data and the main inferences were drawn from it. The secondary data have been collected/consulted just to supplement, clarify and elucidate the primary data and not to supplant them.

The Collection of Data

A considerable field work was carried out by the researcher. After the selection of the sample, the researcher went personally to each and every respondent and recorded the responses to each of the question. The researcher endeavored to meet the child-respondents in their schools and when the respondent was a mother, the researcher made it a point to meet her at the office.

While asking the questions and recording the responses from the respondents, the researcher tried to observe their attitudes, approach, behaviour and the way of speaking. This helped the researcher in gaining the primary as well as secondary information. Finally, the (research) findings were written in an elaborate form, as a report.

Problems in Data Collection

During the course of field work for this study a few problems were faced by the researcher. These problems are mentioned below:

The researcher had to face lot of difficulties while conducting the interview of the children when they were in the Schools/institutions because the authorities seemed averse to it. Some of them bluntly denied permission to the researcher to meet the children and some devised flimsy alibis to keep the researcher away from the children.

A few institutions did allow the researcher to meet the students and conduct the interview but the researcher was required to conduct the interview during the lunch break. The researcher requested the School management to provide the list of the students whose mothers were working. Some institutions simply enquired from the students to provide them the information while as some institutions had kept the record of the same.

It is an onerous job to conduct the interview of the children who are studying. Invariably, the School management had laid the condition that the interview would have to be conducted when the classes were off. Accordingly, the researcher had to meet the respondents during the Lunch break. Unfortunately, the children would be engaged in taking their Lunch and as such only a few children could be interviewed. Many a time the researcher had to wait for the School closure to conduct interview, making the process complicated and time consuming. Often the children were in hurry to be interviewed after the School closure and it was with difficulty that the researcher could persuade some of them for the interview.

The researcher always carried sweets, chocolates and fruits for distribution among the children who were/were to be interviewed. It was intended to make them feel at home and it made the work easier.

It was an arduous task; but the researcher held on, persisted till the completion of the job assigned to the researcher. The researcher recorded all the observations and interviews in a notebook prepared especially for that purpose. This way or that way the researcher got questions answered.

4

FINDINGS OF THE STUDY

I: Problems of children of working women from the Age-Group of 4 months to 4 years :

Findings of the Study-I

There is an enormous amount of hard work in child care: preparing the proper diet, washing clothes, changing diapers, cleaning up messes that an infant makes with food and an older child makes with play, stopping fights and drying tears, listening to stories that are hard to understand, joining in games and reading books that are not very exciting to an adult and responding to pleas for help with the home work. Keeping the child up to the mark and disciplined and making arrangements for child care while the mother is away, is a difficult task. Most of the people love children above everything else and seeing them grow and develop into cultured people, gives most parents — despite the hard work involved in their bringing up — greatest satisfaction in life. Pride in other worldly accomplishments appears as a trifle in comparison.

A very particular need of young children is perseverance of their care givers. From the age of a few months, they come to love and to count on and get their security from one or two people who take the major responsibility of their care. Even a few months old babies will develop serious depression, which is reflected in appetite and interest in things and people if the parents who had cared for them, disappear. So, when the mother is working women a substitute should gradually take over so that the baby does not feel it much and gets used to the new care giver imperceptibly.

The parents should find a person or arrange a relative, who shows much the same kind of love, interest, responsiveness and control as they do. Keeping all these issues in mind it becomes important to find out the problems of the children, while the mothers are away at home.

It has been assumed that the children, whose mothers are working outside their homes, are somehow affected (physically, emotionally, and psychologically). To find out in what way are these children affected, the researcher met these children personally and asked them questions on the basis of the interview schedule already prepared for the purpose. Direct interaction couldn't be held with the children who were below 4 years of age so the researcher interacted with their mothers and enquired from them regarding the various aspects of the life styles and living habits of these children. However, the fact remains that the problems faced by the children who are below the age of 4 years.

Keeping in view the peculiar nature of the study, a separate interview schedule was prepared for the purpose which was designed after taking into consideration the particular perspective of the working mothers regarding their children. The below mentioned tables record the responses of the working mothers of the children who were not considered mature enough to be interviewed.

TABLE 4.1

Care of children during office time

S.No	Responses	Number	%age
a	Your in-laws.	18	18.00
b	Your parents.	38	38.00
c	Servant/Maid.	37	37.00
d	Crèche	07	07
d	Take along with you.	None	0
e	Any other.	None	0
Total		100	100

As is evident from the Table 4.1, majority of the respondents i.e. 38% responded that their children were taken care of by their parents (mothers' parents) while they are at work (mothers have to drop and pick-up the child from their parental home which is itself a problem). 37% respondents said that they left their children with servants/maids during day time while 18% children of the respondents were taken care of by their in-laws (mothers in-laws) and 7% children were in crèches (crèches are coming into being but are not available in all localities, and it is very difficult to pick and drop the child in the crèches).

Thus it can be inferred that majority of the children were looked after by those persons who had no blood relationship with the children like servants and crèches and it is easy to guess that the kind of attention and care received by these children would be, by and large, formal and impersonal and the atmosphere of a loving relationship would be lacking. The effects of such a relationship wouldn't be conducive for the emotional development of a child.

TABLE 4.2

Satisfaction of mother to the day care arrangement

S.No	Responses	Number	%age
a	Yes.	57	57.00
b	No.	38	38.00
c	To some extent.	05	5.00
Total		100	100

To get a clear picture about the day- care arrangement and the satisfaction of mother about it, the respondents were further asked whether they were satisfied with such arrangement for their children. Their statements revealed as indicated in the Table 4.2 that 57% respondents were satisfied with the day care arrangement. 38% respondents were not satisfied and 5% were indecisive in their opinions.

TABLE 4.3

Reasons for being satisfied with the day care arrangement

S.No	Reasons	Number	%age
a	(Others) can do it properly	14	25.00
b	No other alternative	43	75.00
c	(Others) can understand them	None	0
d	Any other reason	None	0
Total		57	100

As is clear from the Table 4.3 that majority of the respondents 75% replied that they have no other alternative except to leave the child to the supervision of another person while 25% thought that others (grand parents, servants) can take care of them (children) properly.

Though 57% affirmed that they were satisfied with the arrangement of day care, yet the researcher concluded by their diffidence and through observation that they were satisfied because they had to be as they had no other option.

TABLE 4.4

Reasons for not being satisfied with the day care arrangement

S.No	Reasons	Number	%age
a	(Others) Don't understand his needs properly	17	44.74
b	(Others) are not interested in them.	21	55.26
c	Any other reason	None	0
Total		38	100

As it is clear from the Table 4.4, majority i.e. 55.26% of the respondents thought that others (grand parents, servants) are not interested in their children as a mother has while 44.74% respondents thought that others can't understand their children's needs properly. This fact needs no arguments. Nobody can contest the fact that nobody, even the best trained psychoanalysts, can comprehend the problems of a child in a better way than a mother. So the ill effects of the *others'* bringing up the child can't be ruled out.

TABLE 4.5

Time leaving for office

S.No	Responses	Number	%age
a	8 AM.	06	06.00
b	9 AM	87	87.00
c	10 AM.	07	07.00
Total		100	100

The respondents were asked when they leave for work, as is depicted in the Table 4.5, majority of the respondents i.e. 87% leave for office at 9AM., 7% respondents leave for office at 10 AM. while 6% at 8 AM.

TABLE 4.6

Preparation for leaving for the office

S.No	Responses	Number	% age
a	7AM.	15	15.00
b	8AM.	81	81.00
c	9AM.	04	04.00
Total	100	100	

Further the respondents were asked when they started preparing for office work. 15% respondents responded that they started preparing for office at 7AM. 81% responded that they started preparing for office at 8AM. And 04% responded that they started preparing for office at 9AM.

The morning time is essential for a child. He had to be dressed, diapered, feed etc. Some mothers would leave home when their children were asleep. It can be inferred that such children would feel disgusted when they wouldn't find their mothers around when they have got up from sleep.

TABLE 4.7

Time spends with the children

S.No.	Responses	Number	%age
a	Yes	04	04.00
b	No	96	96.00
c	Indifferent	None	0
Total		100	100

The respondents were asked whether they get sufficient time to attend to their children. As shown in the analysis (Table 4.7), majority of the respondents i.e. 96% didn't get sufficient time to attend to their children while 04% respondents were satisfied with the time they spend with their children.

TABLE 4.8

Reasons for not spending sufficient time with the children

S.No	Reasons	Number	%age
a	Stay outside home	66	68.75
b	Have to attend domestic duties.	23	23.95
c	After returning back are not in a position to attend children?	07	7.30
d	Any other reason.	None	0
Total		96	100

Further the respondents were asked to report why didn't have they time to spend with their children. As it is evident from the (Table 4.8) 68.75% respondents replied that they had to stay outside homes for major part of the day. 23.95% respondents reported that they had to attend domestic duties after returning from the office. And 07.30% respondents responded that after returning they were not in a position to attend to their children.

TABLE 4.9

Respondents satisfaction for spending time with the children

S.No	Responses	Number	%age
a	Yes	17	17.00
b	No	76	76.00
c	To some extent	07	07.00
Total		100	100

The respondents were asked to report whether or not they were satisfied with the time they spend with their children. As shown in the (Table 4.9) 17% respondents were satisfied. There were 76% respondents who were unsatisfied whereas 07% respondents were not clear in their responses.

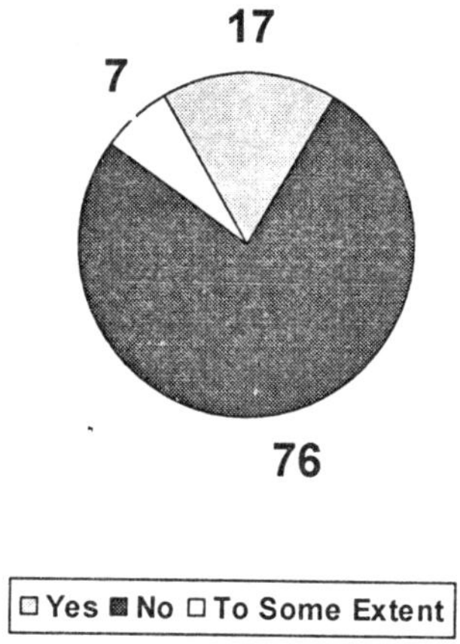

Fig 4.1

Being just, nobody can deny that working women have to shoulder a lot of responsibilities. As the time available for everyone is fixed, a large chunk of the working women's time is spend on her job, which leaves her short time for her children

As recorded above 17% women were satisfied with the time spend with their children, the rest are not, which makes us realise the gravity of the problem.

The responses to the above set of time related questions make it clear that going to and preparing for office leaves but short span of time in the hands of working women which might affect the physical and mental development of the child. Most of the working women start preparing for office from very early in the morning. Obviously, they would not be able to attend to their children even if they (children) were calling for the same. And many a time - the researcher observed during the course of the study - the children would be deliberately taken away during the time their mothers were preparing for their office. A child usually cries for attention when he sees his mother indifferently preparing for office. This indifference on the part of their mothers would be hard upon the psyche of these children.

The time is ticking away but a mother has no choice, she has to attend to her office.

TABLE 4.10

Dietary behaviour of children

S.No	Responses	Number	%age
	Do you feed your child before going for work or entrust it to anybody else?		
a	Yes, feed him/her yourself.	86	86.00
b	No, entrust someone else.	14	14.00
Total		100	100

The respondents were asked to report whether they fed their children before going for office or not, majority 86% respondents as depicted in the Table 4.10, fed their children themselves and 14% entrusted the work to somebody else.

TABLE 4.11

Feeding of children before the proper time

S.No	Responses	Number	%age
a	Yes	60	69.77
b	No	26	30.23
c	Indifferent	none	0
Total		86	100

The respondents, who fed their children themselves, were asked to report whether or not they fed their children at the proper time as they had to leave their homes earlier to attend to their office work. It came to the fore that 69.77% respondents fed their children before the required time. 30.23% were satisfied with the feeding of their children.

TABLE 4.12

Mothers' satisfaction towards the children's' feeding

S.No	Responses	Number	%age
a	Satisfied	54	54.00
b	Over-feed	08	08.00
c	Under-feed	38	38.00
Total		100	100

When the respondents were asked about the eating schedule of their children, 54% were satisfied with the feeding, 8% over-feed their children and 38% under-feed their children.

38% of the respondents confessed that their children didn't get required diet while 8% said that they over-feed their children. The reasons behind over-feeding were obvious: that they (mothers' feared that during the day time their children) would have nothing to eat, so in order that they might eat be starved, they over-fed them and children were under-feed for they couldn't eat properly when they had no appetite. In both the cases, the children would suffer physically.

54% mothers were satisfied with the feeding of their children. But it couldn't be ascertained whether their satisfaction was reasonable or not.

TABLE 4.13

Improper feeding affects the health of these children:

S.No	Responses	Number	%age
a	Yes	29	63.00
b	No	08	18.00
c	To some extent	09	19.00
Total		46	100

As is evident from the analysis (Table 4.13), majority of the respondents 29/46 thought that their children's health deteriorates because of over/under feeding while 9/46 respondents children's health involves to some extent and only 8/46 respondents replied that over/under feeding didn't affect the health of their children.

Notwithstanding what the respondents say, the experts contend that such irregular food habits do affect the child's health.

TABLE 4.14

Improper feeding affects the psyche of these children:

S.No	Responses	Number	%age
a	Yes	17	37.00
b	No	18	39.00
c	To some extent	11	24.00
Total		46	100

As is clear from the Table 4.14 that 17/46 respondents thought that their children's psyche was affected by the over/feeding, while 18/46 respondents thought that heir children's psyche didn't affected and 11/46 were indecisive in their opinions.

The responses to the above diet related questions illustrate that the diet habits of children of working mothers are irregular and gives the impression that these irregular feeding schedules, would tell badly upon the health of these children. In some of the families, the duty of feeding of these children is entrusted to someone else. Evidently the 'others' wouldn't take same pains as does a mother in feeding the children—nor would they feel so much bound.

No doubt 86% mothers feed the children themselves, but 68% of them fed their children before the proper time.

(For they have to go to their work- places and, as such, feed them before leaving for office.) 38% of working women felt that they underfed and 8% overfed their children. (Because they are not fed at the proper time) These things show that all is not right with these children. They are affected on this account too. Proper feeding is essential for a growing child; if he doesn't get it, his health would deteriorate. No doubt, working women can afford specially prepared balanced diet for their children, but it would be of no use if not administered properly and according to the schedule.

Breast Feeding and its Effects

Breast-feeding process in which the mother suckles her new born. Milk from human females provides all the nutrients that a baby needs, as well as substances that promotes growth and helps fight infection

During its first days and weeks, a newborn infant normally feeds 8 to 12 times or more in 24 hours. The frequent breast-feeding stimulates the mother's hormonal system to increase milk production. Physicians advise mothers to breast-feed the baby on demand rather than by an hourly schedule. This practice not only ensures that the baby receives the proper nutrition, but also that the mother's milk supply is maintained. Milk at the beginning of a feeding session is different in composition than milk at the end—the hind milk or later milk which is much richer in fats. Doctors recommend that a breast-feeding session should begin and continue on one breast until the baby spontaneously stops feeding then the mother should offer the other breast, allowing the baby to feed until completely satisfied. Halting feedings after a predetermined time may prevent the infant from obtaining the extra fat calories in the hind milk necessary for proper growth.

Some pediatricians recommend that infants should be breast-fed for at least the first year of life, and possibly into the second and third years for optimal development. For the first six months of life, the healthy infant needs no food or fluid other than breast milk. Beyond that age, mother's milk should be increasingly supplemented with solid food and other fluids.

Perhaps the most important advantage of breast-feeding is that breast milk provides an infant with significant protection against chronic diseases such as allergies and asthma and infectious diseases including meningitis, diarrhea, ear infections, and pneumonia. The immune components of breast milk constantly alter to meet the infant's need to be protected against new infections. As the infant's own immune system grows more capable, the concentration of antibodies and anti-infection agents in the milk gradually declines.

Breast-feeding facilitates bonding between a mother and infant that is emotionally satisfying to both participants. The mother develops nurturing behaviours. The infant, in turn, learns trust. In this connection, too, some questions were asked to the mother respondents to find out the frequency of breast-feeding among those women and related questions.

TABLE 4.15

Breast feeding of children

S.No	Responses	Number	% age
a	Yes	91	91.00
b	No	09	09.00
c	Indifferent	None	0
Total		100	100

The respondents were asked to reveal whether they breast-fed their children or not. The majority of the respondents i.e. 91% reported that they breast-fed their children. However, 09% replied that they didn't breast–fed their children.

TABLE 4.16

Satisfaction of mother to the breast-feeding of their children

S.No	Responses	Number	%age
a	Yes	04	4.40
b	No	87	95.60
c	Indifferent	None	0
Total		91	100

As is evident from the analysis (Table 4.16), respondents were asked whether they were satisfied with the breast-feeding of their children or not. Majority of them i.e. 95.60 were not satisfied with the breast-feeding of their children, only 4.40% were satisfied with the breast-feeding of their children. Thus it can be inferred that the mother's employment is an impediment for the development of the child.

TABLE 4.17

Reasons for not been able to breast-feed their children

S.No	Responses	Number	%age
a	Stay out side more.	54	62.00
b	Have to attend domestic duties	10	11.49
c	Don't have time.	22	25.28
d	Any other reason.	01	01.14
Total		87	100

As is evident from the Table 4.17, majority of the respondents i.e. 54% were not satisfied with the breast-feeding of their children as they had to stay outside homes for major part of the day, 10% respondents had to attend domestic duties after returning from the work, 22% respondents lacked time (they go early and come late) and 01% didn't give any proper reason. Doctors were consulted regarding this problem. They maintained that frequent breast-feeding stimulates the mother's hormonal system to increase milk production. As the working women lack time to breast-feed their children, their milk stimulating hormones are not released; accordingly they fail to produce sufficient milk.

Whatever the reason, the consequences seem discouraging. It is a matter of concern for all the concerned. The study shows that 87 (95.60%) respondents were not able to breast-feed their children properly. Or in other words, 96% children of working mothers are deprived of this natural blessing. They might remain physically underdeveloped; their immunity system would not develop to the required strength, thus making them susceptible to diseases. The reasons provided by working women show that it can't be helped. They are now getting used to it remorselessly. But the children do suffer silently.

The Unbreakable Chord—of Love

Children need always their mothers and there is no need of clarification because every one is born of a mother and they can understand it in a better way.

Love and affection are the important psychological needs of a child. If the child feels, he is not loved or is unwanted, or if the emotional identification with the parents is disrupted, the growing child may seek substitute companionship or may pass through a period of grave insecurity, frustration and resentment even hatred. In the above few questions, the researcher tried to elicit information from the Working mothers whether they were able to give requisite companionship to their children and satisfied their emotional needs, the researcher found that the situation was grim.

TABLE 4.18

Mothers need during the day

S.No	Responses	Number	%age
a	Yes	97	97.00
b	No	02	02.00
c	Indifferent	01	01.00
Total		100	100

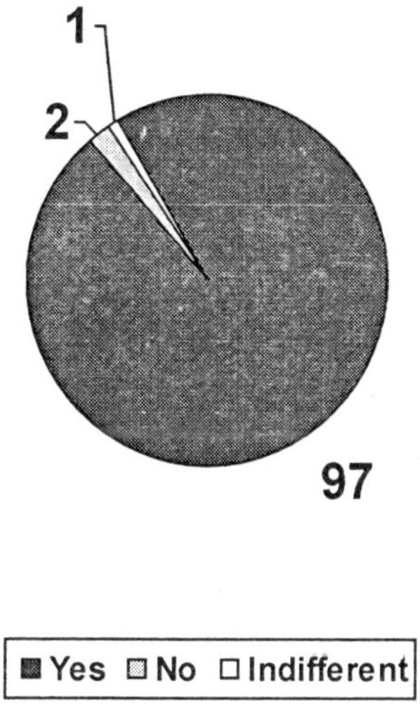

Fig. 4.2

The respondents were asked to report whether they feel that their children needed them during the day or not. Majority i.e. 97% respondents as shown in the Table 4.18, informed that their children needed them during the day as nobody can be a substitute for the mother, 02% informed that they (children) didn't and 01% respondent was indifferent in her response.

TABLE 4.19

Reasons behind the mothers need during the day

S.No	Responses	Number	%age
a	Can feed the child properly	09	9.26
b	Can look after him properly.	05	05.15
c	Others can't take care of a child. as a mother can.	44	45.36
d	Children need mothers always.	39	40.23
Total		97	100

The respondents were asked to report why they (children) need them (mothers) during the day. 46% replied that they thought that others couldn't take care of a child as a mother could, 39% replied that children need mothers always. While 10% respondents reported that they (mothers) could feed them (children) properly. And 05% replied that they could look after them properly.

The above two tables clearly reveal that children need their mothers during the day time when they are at office. Though they provided various reasons, the fact remains undisputable: that there is a void in the life of a child which can be filled only by a mother.

37.83% mothers (39 out of 97) gave a simple reason for the child needing a mother during the day time: that the children needed mothers always. On its face, it appears to be the simplest answer, but it has a sea deep depth in it: that there is an unbreakable bond between the two — that must remain intact.

Under the Shadow of Compassionate Mother

Presence is the best way of tucking love into pockets of time, working mothers should understand how to make their presence qualitatively meaningful. The lowest level of meaningful presence is mental closeness: Letting the person know that you are thinking about him even though you are away. A person may not be physically close to you but you can have them in your thoughts. This is an important way of communicating the message of presence. A few questions were asked to find out whether, after returning from work, a mother could spare time for her children or not.

TABLE 4.20

Attention to the child after returning from the office

S.No	Responses	Number	%age
a	Yes	06	06.00
b	No	88	88.00
c	sometimes	06	06.00
Total		100	100

As is evident from the Table 4.20, majority of the respondents i.e. 88%, after returning from office were not in a position to attend children while 6% respondents replied that they were and 6% respondents responded that sometimes they were in a position to attend children after returning from the office.

TABLE 4.21

Reasons for inattention towards the children:

S.No	Responses	Number	%age
a	Because of fatigue	46	48.94
b	Because of domestic duties.	21	22.34
c	Sufficient time is not available	27	28.72
d	Any other reason.	None	0
Total		94	100

When asked the reasons for not being able to look after their children, when they had returned from their office,

48.96% respondents replied that fatigue was the reason. 22.34% had to perform domestic duties and 28.72% replied that they simply lacked time.

The responses to these questions reveal that it is very difficult for the working women to devote attention to their children properly. Such inattention may create the feeling of being unwanted. Under such circumstances a child may develop bad habits. He might became an introvert and turn to a bad company for solace. And psychologists tell us that such things are the causes of delinquency.

Attention during Illness

During illness children need special attention. This creates problems when the mothers are working. When both parents are working, the responsibility of care for sick children usually falls on the mother.

TABLE 4.22

Care of sick children

S.No	Responses	Number	%age
a	Yourself	65	65.00
b	Your in-laws.	11	11.00
c	Your parents	22	22.00
d	Relatives or friends	02	02.00
e	Servant/Maid.	None	0
Total		100	100

When the respondents were asked to report who takes care of their children when they fall ill, majority of the respondents 65% as is clear from the Table 4.22 responded that they (mothers) look after their children themselves when they are ill (children) while in rest of the cases this responsibility was shared by other agencies such as in-laws, parents (mothers parents), and other relatives and friends.

As for the researcher could infer; the children of working mothers suffer most when they are ill. No doubt 65% respondents attended to their children themselves, but as the researcher looked into their eyes, it transpired that they had a sense of guilt and a profound agony lay deep within the innermost recesses of their hearts. And the researcher realised that no matter whatever the reasons, and in what way they might justify themselves, they conceal the truth: a working women can never be satisfied with the care of her sick children. Besides 35% candidly replied that they were unable to attend to their sick children themselves, and entrusted the work to somebody else. And all of them had some kind of guilt which troubled them but couldn't do anything about.

TABLE 4.23

Respondents satisfied to the performance of mothering role

S.No	Responses	Number	%age
a	Yes	46	46.00
b	No	51	51.00
c	To some extent.	03	03.00
Total		100	100

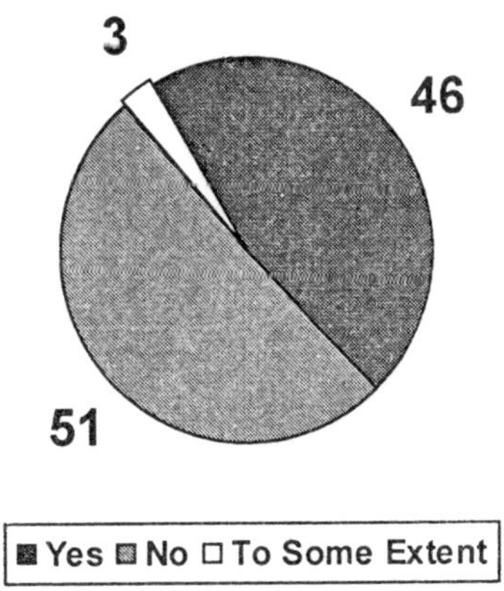

Fig. 4.3

In connection with the performance of mothering role, respondents were further asked to reveal whether they were satisfied with the performance of their mother roles. 46% of the respondents replied that they were, 51% of the respondents were not and 03% were satisfied only to some extent with the performance of their mothering roles.

Most of the women have not yet learned to cope up with their dual responsibilities, but with the passage of time things might change and mothers would learn to do justice with their dual roles.

Consequences of Mother's Absence

There are many seemingly important options which the parents pursue. In our society parenting has been relegated to a rather low-status position because it doesn't measure up on those variables that usually determine status. Working mothers have no choice but to stay away from their children. Based on the absence of mother during the day and the probable problems it might create, following two questions were asked to the mother respondents.

TABLE 4.24

Mothers' absence create problems during the day:

S.No	Responses	Number	%age
a	Yes	61	61.00
b	No	27	27.00
c	To some extent	12	12.00
Total		100	100

The respondents were asked whether they thought that their absence during the day created any problems in their children. The analysis (Table 4.24) shows that 61% respondents felt that it caused problems 27% respondents felt that it didn't and 12% respondents replied it created problems in them (children) to some extent.

TABLE 4.25

Type of problems created by the absence of the mother:

S.No	Responses	Number	%age
a	Health	46	63.10
b	Nutritional	07	9.5
c	Behavioural	20	27.40
d	Any other.	None	0
Total		73	100

When the respondents, who in response to the previous question had said that it did create problems, were asked to report as to what type of problems were created in their children during their (mothers') absence, majority of the respondents i.e.63.10% (Table 4.25) thought that their children's health deteriorated, the children of 09.5% respondents suffered from nutritional problems and the behaviour of the children of 27.40% respondents was affected because of their absence during the day.

The response to the above set of questions makes it clear that the mother's absence does affect their children. Though only 61% admitted that creates problems and 12% admitted that it creates problems occasionally, the researcher or for that matter any keen observer, could infer that the mothers' absence created problems for the children. The problems created are of diverse nature, like health, nutritional and behavioural. Besides, there might be some other types of problems that might have escaped their observation. Of course, 27% respondents claimed that no problem was created, but it might be that the problems might have gone unnoticed or that they might have attributed these problems to some other causes. One thing the researcher could safely deduce was that the absence of mother does certainly cause problems in young children.

(Here the researcher was concerned with children below the age of 4 years)

The interactions with the working mothers reveal that the absence of mothers from their homes has definite repercussions on their children. These effects in the early years of life of a child might leave life long effects on the children. As the psychologists say that the childhood experiences leave their effects throughout the life of a person.

II: Problems of children of working women from the Age-Group of 4 -12 years:

Findings of the Study-II

Child's personality formation and then development takes place as a result of close interaction with the significant others in his environment, where mother comes first, then father and siblings and later a few extra familiar figures. The child brings to his interaction a certain biological constitution, some needs and drives, and some intellectual capacities which determine his reactions to the way in which he is acted upon by these significant others. It is at first the family structure, pattern and the system and family environment that influences the child's development (Physical, intellectual, emotional and social).

Family in a society occupies the central place around which human activities—social and economic—revolve around in such a way so that human survival becomes possible. It is in this context that role of family in socialization process has been recognised beyond doubt. Essentially, the family as a group consists of a mother, a father and siblings. The first education of the child therefore takes place in his contact with the family. Inheriting a certain culture, understanding specific values and coming to terms with the immediate surrounding are areas where the child is influenced the most by the family. The responsibilities for the psychological and emotional welfare of the child closely follow. It is only within the family that the child gets his lesson in social learning. The family, into which a child is born, is one of the major determinants of his subsequent success in school.

Family occupies a unique place in the development of the individual. First is the group which, is virtually common to all human experiences with a small minority of exceptions, every child is born into a family group and lives in a family for a considerable period of time. Second, the child has his earliest experiences in a family setting and his interpretation of these experiences will influence all his later perceptions. When he encounters some novel relationship in adult life, he is likely to act on the basis of some apparent similarity to an experience of early life.

The mother, of course, plays a very important role in the child's development. She gives affection and dispenses discipline; she rewards and punishes the child. Furthermore, she serves as model which the child imitates. When there is a discrepancy between mother's instructions and behaviours, the child is prone to follow the latter. Thus, the mother is the major determinant of the hopes, fears and expectations of the child.

Let us investigate the findings given below and chart out how children of working women are affected (from the age-group of 4-12 years) and how they fare under such circumstances.

Preparation for the School

Every child wants that his/her mother prepare him/her for the school; He/she is by birth attached to his/her mother. Out of both parents mother is more close to her child. A child always wishes that her mother were with him/her, but when the mother is working outside home then it is not possible that she remains around the child all the time. Every human being is in need of attention and a child needs it more. Mother is the first person who can attend to or give attention to the child more than any body else can.

TABLE 4.26

Preparation for the school

S.No	Responses	Number	%age
a	Mother.	97	48.5
b	Father.	03	1.5
c	Grand parents.	05	2.5
d	Servant/maid.	12	6.00
e	Any other.	None	0
f	Prepare on your own.	83	41.5
Total		200	100

The respondents were asked to report who prepared them for the school. As shown in the (Table 4.26) majority of the respondents 48.5% replied that their mothers prepared them for the school. The substantial proportion of the respondents 41% were prepared themselves for the school, 6% respondents were prepared by servants/maids, 2.5% respondents were by grandparents and 1.5% respondents were prepared for the school by their fathers.

The findings revealed that about one half of the respondents prepared for schools without being helped by anyone. This shows that their mothers had little time to prepare them for the schools. This has positive as well as negative effects.

Positive effects in the sense, it would make the child self dependent.

Negative in the sense, the child would be over burdened. His precious time would be wasted.

The net effect will depend upon the peculiar conditions.

Educational Guidance Outside School

Children are sending to schools for the formal educational guidance. But if the schools are not up to the mark or the teachers in the schools are not teaching them properly, these children need some extra educational guidance at homes.

Sometimes, a teacher advises that a child is falling behind and needs extra tutoring in a subject or the parents get this idea themselves. This extra educational guidance can either on a regular basis or whenever the child needs it. Besides in today's competitive world, every parent wishes that their children carve a niche for themselves in life.

TABLE 4.27

Educational Guidance outside school

S.No	Responses	Number	%age
a	Tutor	106	53.00
b	Father.	27	13.5
c	Mother.	24	12.00
d	Any other	04	2.00
e	No one	39	19.5
Total		200	100

The respondents were asked who teaches them at home. As is evident from the Table 4.27, 53% respondents were going for private tuition, 13.5% respondents were taught by their fathers, 12% respondents were taught by their mothers, 2% respondents replied that any other person taught them. And 19.5% respondents replied that no one taught them. (They were reading in the lower classes).

The findings revealed that the children of the working mothers are taught at the home whether by tutors/ parents. This shows that the children of working mothers are given good education. As data is not available about the children of non- working mothers, so we can't say it properly is there any difference between the educational standard of children of working and non-working mothers.

Mothers' presence in the school function:

Child comes into the world with free mind. At birth, he has no experiences. After taking birth, he comes into contact with human beings, especially mother and imitates the actions of her mother. A child needs attachment/ attention of some one, and when some one shows him any type of interest hė develops emotionally well. Every mother loves her children but a mother needs to show the child in some way that she miss/need her child. A child has not so much capacity to understand the unspoken language of others; they can't feel like an adult. There are many ways through which a mother can convey the child how much she loves her child. School function is one of them.

TABLE 4.28

Mothers' presence in the school function

S.No	Responses	Number	%age
a	Yes	21	10.5
b	No	91	45.5
c	Sometimes	88	44.00
Total		200	100

The respondents were asked to report whether their mothers attend the school functions celebrated in their schools or not. As is evident from the Table 4.28, 45.5% of the respondents' mothers didn't attend the school functions of their children, the substantial proportion of the respondents i.e. 44% replied that sometimes their mothers attended their school functions and 10.5% replied that they (mothers) attended their school functions.

The above findings revealed that majority of the respondents' mothers (89.5%) didn't attend the school functions of their children. This shows that their mothers rarely attended the school functions of their children. Only 21(10.5%) attended their school functions regularly. They (working mothers) miss the chance of giving their children feeling of nearness.

TABLE 4.29

Respondents' attitude towards the mother's absence in school functioning:

S.No	Responses	Number	%age
a	You miss her.	77	43.00
b	You get a feeling of loneliness and desperation.	65	36.35
c	You feel inferiority complex.	30	16.75
d	It does not matter to you.	07	03.90
Total		179	100

When the 179 respondents, whose mothers didn't attend the school functions or do so occasionally, were asked how they feel when their mothers didn't attend their school functions. As is shown in the Table 4.30 43% respondents missed their mothers in the school functions, 36.3% respondents get a feeling of loneliness and desperation, 16.7% respondents suffered from inferiority complex and 4% didn't miss their mothers because their friends were there to play with them.

The above findings revealed that majority of the respondents missed their mothers in their school functions. This is the psychological problem and can't be ignored. Consultation with psychologists, it is found that it will create some psychological problems for these children.

After Returning from School Mother's Presence

Every child wants to rush into the caressing arms of her mother after returning from school. But unfortunately, today's children, when they came from school don't find their mothers at home because the mothers are working outside homes.

TABLE 4.30

After returning from school mothers' presence

S.No	Responses	Number	%age
a	Yes	09	4.5
b	No	131	65.5
c	Sometimes	60	30.00
Total		200	100

The respondents were asked to report whether they found their mothers at home after returning from the school. In this connection 4.5% respondents replied in affirmative, 65.5% respondents replied in negative and 30% respondents replied that some times they (children) found their mothers at homes after returning from the schools.

TABLE 4.31

Respondents' feeling on finding their mothers at home after school

S.No	Responses	Number	%age
a	Happy.	55	79.7
b	Secure.	03	4.3
c	Care free.	11	16.00
d	It makes no difference.	None	0
Total		69	100

The respondents were further asked how they felt, if they found their mothers at home after returning from the school. The analysis (Table 4.26) reveals that 79.7% of the respondents feel happy. 03 4.3% respondents feel secured in presence of their mothers and the rest of the respondents 16% feel care free in presence of their mothers.

TABLE 4.32

Respondents' feeling on not finding their mothers at home after school:

S.No	Responses	Number	%age
a	Wish that she were at home	126	66.00
b	Miss your mother.	63	33.00
c	Do not care about her.	02	01.00
d	Do not miss her.	None	0
Total		191	100

The above findings revealed that 95.5% respondents didn't or occasionally found their mothers at homes after returning from the schools. When these respondents were asked how they feel when they did not found their mothers at home. 66% respondents wished that their mothers would be there after returning from the school. 33% of them missed their mothers and 1% didn't care about the absence of their mothers.

The above set of questions revealed that only 4.5% respondents found their mothers regularly at their homes and 95.5% respondents didn't or occasionally found their mothers at homes after returning from their schools. After returning back they were fatigued and needed their mothers to feed them. It is quite clear that the children face lot of problems when their mothers were not present there at that time. When they returned back from the schools and found there homes empty they felt desperate and wished that their mothers would be there. They needed them to feed them, love them and to give them the feeling of importance.

TABLE 4.33

Respondents' activity on holidays

S.No	Responses	Number	%age
a	Study at home.	61	30.5
b	Study as well as play.	59	29.5
c	Go outside and play	20	10.00
d	Watch T.V. and study	27	13.5
e	Spend time with your parents.	25	12.5
f	Watches T.V.	08	4.00
Total		200	100

The analysis (Table 4.33) reveals that 30.5% respondents studied at home in holidays, 29.5% respondents studied as well as play during the holidays, and 10% respondents go outside and play with the children of their age while 13.5% respondents replied that they watch T.V. after returning from the school 12.5%, respondents spend time with their parents and 4% respondents watch T.V. as well as study on holidays.

It appears that the habits of the children of the working mothers are not deteriorated. They use their time judiciously. Most of them study; there are only 10% who just play and 4% just watch T.V.

Working mothers are mostly well qualified and they wish their children to study too. They instill in their children the habits of reading. Although they do play or watch T.V., but they don't forget to study.

Diet Habits

Human beings require food to grow, reproduce and maintain good health. Eating the rich food helps us avoid certain diseases or recover faster when illness occurs. These and other important functions are fueled by chemical substances in our food called nutrients.

When a person is not provided adequate diet, he suffers from malnutrition: The brain may become sluggish and react slowly. Besides he suffers physical weaknesses.

TABLE 4.34

Feeding of the children in absence of the mother

S.No	Responses	Number	%age
a	Eat the food on your own	69	34.5
b	Servant/ Maid.	62	31.00
c	Elderly siblings	38	19.00
d	Grand parents.	31	15.5
Total		200	100

Attempt was made to find out the feelings of the respondents about the feeding in absence of their mothers, 34.5% replied that they eat the food on their own, 31% respondents replied that servants/maids feed them in absence of their mothers while 19% respondents replied that their elderly siblings feed them during their mothers absence and 15.5% replied that their grand parents feed them during mother's absence.

TABLE 4.35

Respondents' satisfaction/dissatisfaction on being fed by other agencies:

S.No	Responses	Number	%age
a	Yes	121	92.3
b	No	10	7.7
c	Indifferent	None	0
Total		131	100

As shown in the above Table 4.34, 65.5% respondents replied that others fed them during the absence of their mothers and when they were asked did the other agencies fed them properly. 92.3% replied that they fed them properly and only 7.7% respondents replied that they didn't feed them properly.

TABLE 4.36

Comparison of respondents' on being fed by her mother or by other agencies:

S.No	Responses	Number	%age
a	Yes	36	30.00
b	No	06	5.00
c	I feel the absence of my mother	79	65.00
Total		121	100

When these 121 respondents, who were fed by other agencies were asked whether other agencies, apart from mothers, feed them as good as their mothers, 30% respondents replied that they fed them as good as their mothers, 5% respondent were not satisfied with the feeding of other agencies and 65% respondents feel the absence of their mothers during feeding time.

Notwithstanding the fact that 60.5% respondents admitted that other agencies feed them properly, yet majority of them confessed that they were not satisfied with others feeding them. The same respondents had admitted in the previous question that others fed them properly but in the following question they revealed that they were not 'satisfied'. On the face of it, it appears a contradictory statement. But when one attached exact meaning to the words, the word 'satisfaction' has a psychological connotation; it denotes a state of mind rather than of physical necessities. The word 'properly' means that all the material needs are fulfilled. By saying that 'others fed them properly' they wanted to convey that others didn't make any lapse in feeding them. But when they said that they were not satisfied they wanted to convey that something beyond material existence was lacking when they fed them.

It can be inferred that there certainly is a difference between the feeding of a mother and that of others. The feeding of mother is a blend of eatables and maternal love while as the feeding by others is lacking or insufficient on this front.

Health

Physical fitness is usually measured in relation to functional expectations—that is, typically, by periodic tests measuring strength, endurance, agility, coordination, and flexibility. In addition, stress testing, which ascertains the body's accommodation to powerful, sustained physical stimuli, is used to analyze fitness. If individuals are able to accommodate to the stressors, they are assumed to be fit.

TABLE 4.37

Care of children during illness

S.No	Responses	Number	%age
a	Mother.	118	59.00
b	Father.	13	6.5
c	Grand parents.	12	06.00
d	Servant/ maid.	17	08.5
e	Both mother and father.	40	20
Total		200	100

The respondents were asked who takes care of them when they fell ill, as is depicted in the Table 4.37, 59% respondents were taken care of by their mothers during illness, 6.5% respondents were by their fathers, 6% respondents were taken care of by their grand parents and 8.5% respondents were taken care by the servants/maids and 20% respondents replied that both fathers and mothers took care of them during their illness.

The above findings revealed that majority (79%) respondents were taken care of by their parents. It is better for the emotional development of the child.

TABLE 4.38

Mothers' going to office or staying at home during the child's illness

S.No	Responses	Number	%age
a	Yes	72	36.00
b	No	110	55.00
c	Indifferent	18	09.00
Total		200	100

The respondents were asked to report whether their mothers' go to the office or not when they fell ill. As indicated in Table 4.38, 36% respondents' mothers go to the office during their children's illness (other agencies are there to look after them during illness), 55% respondents' mothers didn't and 9% respondents were indifferent in their approaches.

TABLE 4.39

Need of mother during illness

S.No	Responses	Number	%age
a	Yes	200	100.00
b	No	None	0
c	Indifferent	None	0
Total		200	100

The respondents were asked to report whether they wished that their mothers were with them during their illness or not. All the 200 (100%) respondents replied that they wished that their mothers were with them during their (children's) illness.

TABLE 4.40

Reasons for need of mothers' presence during illness

S.No	Responses	Number	%age
a	She understands your problem better than others.	101	50.5
b	Feel secure in presence of your mother	65	32.5
c	Get a feeling of loneliness in absence of mother.	28	14.00
d	You just want your mother around.	06	3.00
Total		200	100

As is evident from the Table 4.40, 50.5% respondents replied that their mothers could understand their problems better than any body else, 32.5% respondents felt secure in presence of their mothers, 14% respondents get a feeling of loneliness in absence of their mothers and 03% respondents replied that during illness they only want their mothers to be around.

The above findings (Table 4.39) revealed that all the 200 respondents were of the view that they wished that their mothers should be there during illness; though they provided different reasons for wishing their mothers to be with them. The message is unambiguous: children need their mothers always. During illness they need them more because it is only mother who can take care of a child in a proper way. No other person can take the place of the mother. It is natural, but when the children are conditioned to live without their mothers they might think it natural, yet it is not a natural way of life. The illness brings forth the natural instincts of a child and he yearns for the natural order of things.

Child care during Mothers' Absence

Home care is excellent for younger children who find it difficult to adjust to new situations. Baby sitters are usually paid to watch, play with and care for the children, so the children should receive their sitter's full attention.

If the care-giver doesn't like the child whom he is caring for (or doesn't like children in general) this attitude will be reflected in the child's feelings about himself. If a caregiver disciplines a child in a way that generates the feelings of guilt or shame, this diminishes a child's self-concept. If the care giver doesn't meet the child's needs for love and attention, a young child often feels that he or she is at fault. This feeling can spread and the child may even erroneously reason that he is to blame for his parent's absence. He may believe that they leave him because they don't like him or enjoy being with him. Thus, his self-concept is further diminished.

TABLE 4.41

Child care during mothers' absence:

S.No	Responses	Number	%age
a	Grand parents.	35	17.5
b	Elder and grown-up siblings.	45	22.5
c	Servant /maid at home.	63	31.5
d	Baby sitter at the day care centre.	None	0
e	No one	57	28.5
Total		200	100

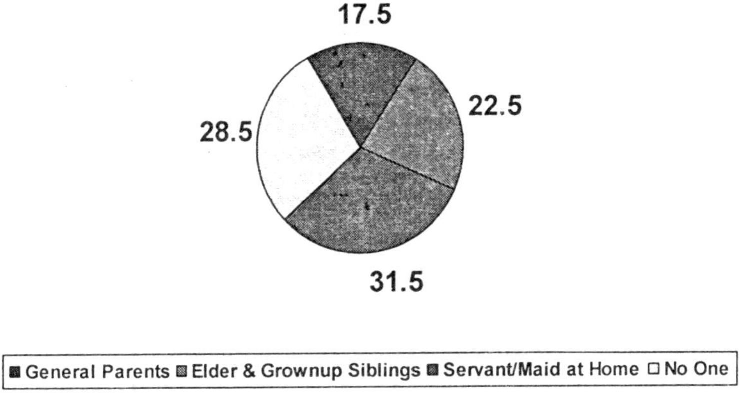

Fig 4.4

The respondents were asked who takes care of them during the absence of their mothers. 17.5% respondents replied that their grandparents take care of them. 22.5% respondents replied that their elderly and grown-up siblings, 31.5% respondents replied that their servants/ maids took care of them during the absence of their mothers and 28.5% respondents replied that they were taken care by no one (as they were grown ups)

TABLE 4.42

Respondents' feelings towards the other agencies looking after their children in absence on their mothers:

S.No	Responses	Number	%age
a	Like him/her.	124	86.7
b	Don't like him/her	18	12.6
c	Hate him/her.	01	0.7
d	Like him/her more than your mother	None	0
Total		143	100

The respondents were asked what they felt about the person who looked after them. As is shown in the Table

4.42, 86.6% respondents liked those persons who looked after them while 12.6% respondents didn't like the persons who looked after them during the absence of their mothers and 0.7% respondent hated the person who looked after him during the absence of her mother.

It is human nature to adjust in the given environment. So, it is a good trend that the children of working mothers are getting adjusted with others (grand parents, servants/ maids etc.)

Activity of working women after returning from office (as revealed by their children):

A working women obviously plays a double role; the traditional feminine role of a house wife/mother or daughter and that of a worker. Her role as a house wife/ office worker often takes up a lot of her physical and mental energy and leaves very little strength to invest in her role as a mother, except for working in the office for a stipulated number of hours. She has her own problems and can't spend time with her children.

TABLE 4.43

Activity of working women after returning from office (as revealed by their children):

S.No	Responses	Number	%age
a	Attends to house-hold chores.	132	66.00
b	Spends time with you and do the household chores.	49	24.5
c	Take rest.	11	5.5
d	Spends time with you	08	04.00
Total		200	100

The respondents were asked to reveal what their mothers did when they returned from the office, 66%

respondents mothers attended to the household chores, 24.5% respondents replied that their mothers, after returning from the office, attended to them & also attended the household chores while 5.5% respondents mothers take rest and 4% of respondents replied that their mothers spent time with them after returning from the office.

The above findings revealed that majority of the respondents' mothers were not attending their children after returning from the office. As it is shown above they have to, after returning back from office, attend domestic duties. The mothers of such children have no time to spend with their children. How can their children develop psychologically/physically? Presence is the best way of communicating the feeling of love, affection, importance; as psychologists also stressed the importance of closeness. For the development of a child closeness is important. But, unfortunately, working mothers are unable to give their children the message of nearness.

TABLE 4.44

Mothers' appearance after returning from office:

S.No	Responses	Number	%age
a	Exhausted.	162	81.00
b	Happy.	24	12.00
c	Bad tempered.	08	4.00
d	Upset.	06	3.00
Total		200	100

The respondents in the Table 4.44 were asked when their mothers returned from office how they found their mothers. 81% respondents found their mothers exhausted, 12% respondents found their mothers happy, 4% respondents found their mothers bad tempered and 3%

respondents found their mothers upset when they returned from the office.

As is evident from the Table 4.44 and as can be realized from day-to-day experience, working mothers are exhausted after returning from their office. This fact was confirmed by 81% of the respondents. The degree of fatigue was so much that they couldn't conceal it even from the eyes of their children.

No doubt, some women might get satisfaction/ contentment from their work, but that wouldn't by any means mean that they are not exhausted. Besides, the study bore it out: only 15.5% respondents narrated that they felt their mothers happy after they returned from the office.

The exhaustion might make the working women indifferent to their children or render them unable to attend to their children, not only this, as is mentioned elsewhere in the study (Table 4.43) most of the working women have to attend to their domestic chores after returning from the office making their work even more troublesome.

TABLE 4.45

Time spends by working women outside home (as revealed by their children):

S.No	Responses	Number	%age
a	Four – Six hours.	18	09.00
b	Six— Eight hours.	168	84.00
c	More than eight hours.	14	07.00
Total		200	100

The respondents were asked how long did their mothers stay outside the homes. As is evident from the Table 4.45, 9% respondents said that their mothers stayed outside homes for four to six hours while 84% respondents replied that their mothers stayed outside homes for six to eight hours and 7% respondents replied that their mothers stayed outside homes more than eight hours.

A working mother spends more than half of her day outside the home. A working woman, who remains outside home for about eight hours, would find it hard to cater to the needs of her family. She can't fulfill the demands of her family and as such the bad affects are going to be reflected in the behaviour of their children.

TABLE 4.46

Activities performed by working women on holidays:

S.No	Responses	Number	%age
a	Attends to house-hold chores.	155	77.5
b	Takes care of you and attends house hold chores.	40	20.00
c	Spends time with you	05	2.5
d	Goes outside home.	None	0
Total		200	100

The respondents were asked what their mothers did on holidays. As is depicted in the Table 4.46, majority i.e. 77.5% of the respondents' mothers attended the household chores on holidays while 20% respondents' mothers did the household chores and also attended them and 2.5% respondents replied that on holidays their mothers just spend time with them on holidays.

Most of the working mothers have other things to attend on holidays. The fact that 77.5% respondents' mothers attend the domestic work on holidays speaks volumes in the fact. Only 20% women are able to attend to their children as well as do the domestic work, on holidays, shows the grimness of the problem.

Usually on holidays the working mothers tidy up their messed homes, which leave them little time to attend to their children. The mothers' of these children might be wishing to attend to their children, but they are called upon to attend to other inevitable jobs, leaving their children to fend for themselves.

TABLE 4.47

Outings with mothers'

S.No	Responses	Number	%age
a	Yes	76	38.00
b	No	50	25.00
c	Sometimes	74	37.00
Total		200	100

The respondents were asked whether their mothers go to the outings with them or not. 38% respondents replied that their mothers go to the outings with them (children) while 25% respondents' mothers did not and 37% respondents' mothers go to the outings with them occasionally.

The analysis (Table 4.47) shows that only 25% of working women don't take their children on outings which show a healthy trend among working women.

Taking children on outings may produce healthy results. They (children) might get a chance of seeing the outside world and meet new faces, which might add up to their personality.

TABLE 4.48

Grievance of children against mothers' job

S.No	Responses	Number	%age
a	Yes	43	21.5
b	No	134	67.00
c	Indifferent	23	11.5
Total		200	100

The respondents were asked whether they felt happy or not if their mothers gave up their jobs. 21.5% respondents replied that they would felt happy if their mothers' gave up their jobs, 67% respondents were not in favour of their mothers' giving up their jobs and 11.5% respondents were indifferent in their approaches.

It can be inferred from the analysis (Table 4.48) that the children have got used to the working of their mothers and the routine of their job. It appears that though the children face problems but they are not aware of its underlying causes. They would like to maintain status quo. Any disturbance in it might produce harmful effects. It might doom their happiness if they were to see their mothers giving up their jobs and change their life style.

Socialization

Man is not only social but also cultural being. It is the culture that provides opportunities for man to develop his personality traits. Development of personality is not an automatic process. Every society prescribes its own ways and means of giving social training to its new born members so that they may develop their own personality. This social training is called 'socialization'.

The process of socialization is conditioned by culture. Every society has its own culture the ways of the process of socialization also differ from society to society. The same culture and the same ways of socialization may have diverse effects on the development of the personality of the members of the same society.

The respondents were asked when they committed any mistake or misbehaved what was the response of their mothers. 87% respondents were of the response that their mothers advised them to behave with others properly. 7.5% respondents answered that their mothers shouted at them when they (children) did any type of mischief and 5.5% respondents replied that their mothers beat them up for misbehaving.

TABLE 4.49

Mothers' attitude towards respondent's misbehaviour:

S.No	Responses	Number	%age
a	Advises you how to behave with others.	174	87.00
b	Shouts at you.	15	07.5
c	Beats you.	11	5.5
d	Kisses and hugs you	None	0
Total		200	100

It can be deduced from the figures that the working women are refined women. As most of them (mothers) (87%) advise their children how to behave with elders. A small portion (7.5%) shouts at them and (5.5%) beats their children.

It has been observed that advising a child on behavioural norms is more effective than using stern methods. The researcher also observed that most of the non-working mothers use rough and tough methods with their children. The long term effects of such behaviour might be detrimental to the social development of the child.

TABLE 4.50

The agencies guiding children in their behaviour:

S.No	Responses	Number	%age
a	Father	28	14.00
b	Mother	76	38.00
c	Both mother and father.	94	47.00
d	Grand parents	02	01.00
e	Servant /maid at home	None	0
f	Elder and grown-up siblings.	None	0
Total		200	100

The respondents were asked who taught them how to behave with elders. As is evident from the Table 4.50, 14% respondents replied that their fathers taught them how to behave with others, 38% respondents replied that their mothers while 47% respondents answered that both mothers and fathers taught them to behave with elders in a good manner and 01% respondents grandparents taught them how to behave with elders.

The task shows that only 30 (28+2) children are those who are not taught the ways of behaviour by their mothers. In case of the rest the mothers appears to be instrumental in leading the children the lesson on behaviour 76 (35%) are those who are exclusively taught the ways of behaviour by their mothers.

It is evident from the task, as well as from the inferred observation which the researcher made that the working mothers make the behavioural training of their children incumbent upon them. The reason might be that they know it from outside home experience that the behaviour with elders is of utmost importance in the personality of their children. Consequently, they take pains to inculcate such values in their children.

Mothers' company is essential for socialization of their children. It is evident no working women pay their full attention to their children because of time constraint. It might create some social/psychological problems for them.

5

CONCLUSION

Conclusion is the final result or the judgment reached by reasoning. It is the summing up of an argument or a book. In the research programmes, conclusions are drawn after the interpretation and analysis of the data collected. On the basis of these conclusions or inferences we derive generalizations about the total population from which the sample for the study has been taken, scientific conclusions are not particularistic, but general in nature. They are not related to the specific or unique characteristics or behaviours of the individual. As such the conclusions drawn about them cover not only the individuals who have been studied but also the similar individuals who were not selected in the sample. The generalizations arrived at through the conclusions. Thus, cover groups or classes irrespective of place and time. Conclusions are, as such, the cumulative analysis of all the findings of the research.

In our society the care and bringing up of children is considered primarily the responsibility of the mother. Sometimes the decision to take up employment depends upon this critical factor. Bringing up of children is a difficult job. Home keeping and child rearing is almost a complete profession and working mother can only pursue it successfully if she gets a close co-operation from her husband or in-laws. In case desired co-operation is not available, she fails to provide an environment of affection, protection and security to her child. Being tired of the outside work she gets irritated and out of irritation punishes her child unnecessarily. Sometimes they suffer from a sense of guilt because they feel that their mothers neglect them because of their outside work.

Working women is a hard reality of modern life. The economic conditions of today force women to opt for working outside their homes. The result is that their children suffer from various socio-psychological problems. There is no one to relate their woes to and they suffer silently. We can't revert to our past tradition, where the women were confined to their homes and played with their children, so we must devise some alternative means to mitigate the sufferings of these children.

Right from the beginning of the civilization, the women have remained confined to their homes. Traditionally they were assigned with the work of home making. However, under the impact of industrialization and later given imputes it was by World War II, which took men to frontiers to fight and left women behind. The women began engaging in gainful employment. Women's work was also necessitated by rising living costs and insufficiency of men folk to manage fully the various activities which are a part of today's fast moving industrial world.

Under the impact of the western culture, Indian culture too assimilated this cultural trait, and slowly women in large numbers began working. Thus, a new type of culture came into existence. The transformation in Kashmiri culture was sudden. Within a single generation, a whole lot of women began working. However, this was not without correlates. It demanded a change in our whole social set up, which were slow to come. Consequently, the effects were felt on other social structures. And as the researcher investigated, the children of these women are definitely affected.

The present study has been divided into following four chapters:

1. Introduction including Review of Literature.
2. Methodology.
3. Findings of the study.
4. Conclusion and suggestions.

In the first chapter "Introduction" humble attempt has been made to unfold the causes that lead women to work outside home and the circumstances which made the socio-cultural factors conducive to women's work.

As a preliminary step the researcher made an exhaustive study of various books, Journals, News Papers, articles and other articles from internet regarding the impact of mother's employment on their children.

The inferences drawn from these sources are also a part of the first chapter. Later on these studies acted as a guide to the researcher and made her work comprehensible. In the first chapter attempt has also been made to Review the Literature which the researcher came upon and which appeared to be of immense value on the topic. The studies focus on the effects of women's outside work on their children. Some scholars have directly dwelled upon the problems suffered by the children whose mothers are working. While as some scholars have made indirect references; like the role conflict among women and the problems encountered by working women while bringing up their children and the consequences of it on their children. They also seek to examine the emotional and psychological aspects of the problems suffered by these children or in other words they have tried to examine how far the psyche of these children affected.

The second chapter, "Methodology" deals with the methods and techniques employed by the researcher to collect the relevant data and put it into usable form. The methods used were interview schedule and observation method. The study was conducted on a sample consisting of 300 respondents. Out of these three hundred respondents, 100 respondents were the mothers of those children who were below the age of 4 years and 200 respondents were children from the age-group of 4-12 years. So a systematic and methodological attempt was made for achieving the objectives of the study.

The third chapter is the "Findings of the study". It makes an exposition of the various facets of the study. The empirical data has been put into tabular form and conclusions regarding various propositions have been drawn.

The final chapter (the present one) draws the comprehensive conclusion from the whole study.

The present study involved into two entities:

1. Problems of children of working women from the Age-Group of 4months to 4 years:
2. Problems of children of working women from the Age-Group of 4 to 12 years:

Therefore, it is imperative to analyze the problem through two perspectives. One was to analyze it through the analysis of problems as it appeared to mothers and second was to analyze it through the perception of children, who are the actual sufferers.

Therefore a set of two interview schedules, specific to each entity, was formulated and besides the input from other sources was also added to arrive at the final conclusions.

In this chapter the summary of all the findings has been presented. The conclusion which emerged from the findings has been outlined as under:

I: Problems of children of working women from the Age-Group of 4months to 4 years:

The working women are mostly qualified and have good income. These things would definitely prove beneficial. But these things are not exclusive to the working women. Others can also be well qualified and have good income. Therefore, these things can't be taken into consideration as an exclusive thing about working women.

Majority of the respondents children were taken care of by their grand parents during their mothers' absence.

Majority of the respondents i.e. 57% were satisfied with the day care arrangement a substantial proportion 38% were not satisfied with this arrangement and a little 5% were satisfied to some extent.

Out of the satisfied respondents (57), 43 respondents said that they had no other alternative except to leave the child in some body else's supervision while 14 respondents just had a thought that others can take care of a child properly in their absence.

From the above findings it may be concluded that mostly the respondents were satisfied with the care takers who take care of their children. The working mothers felt sense of guilt at the thought that their children didn't receive proper care. In other words, they are solacing themselves that they are satisfied with the person who is taking care of their children.

Majority of the respondents i.e. 96% confessed that they didn't get sufficient time to spend with their children. The problem was more acute when the children are not going to school. It transpired that sometimes it was the respondents' in-laws, sometimes it was the respondents' parents and sometimes it was the servant/maid who looked after such children.

Now the problem is whether these (other people) take same pains as the mothers do or not? The answer is clear "No". For the proper care of a child there is need of emotional attachment. And others' have not such attachment with a child as a mother has.

Majority of the respondents, i.e. 86% feed their children before going for the office. And as a necessity they were to be fed before time and often are under/over feed. Though some mothers felt that it was alright, but it was definitely going to affect their health badly.

Majority of the respondents i.e. 95.60% were not able to breast feed their children properly which too was a cause of worry. The reason behind it is time constraint.

Majority i.e. (97%) mothers confessed that their children need them during the day. Lend credence to the proposition that there can be substitute for a mother. The children whose mothers are not working have one advantage that at least they enjoy the company of their mothers when they return from the schools as majority of the children of working women don't enjoy this advantage. Even on holidays working women don't have time for their children they are engaging in various vocations.

Even when the mothers return from the office majority i.e., 94% are not in a position to attend their children. As it is evident that due to various reasons, they are either fatigued, have to attend domestic chores or simply don't have time. These things would definitely affect the child. A relationship of communion wouldn't be established. Therefore, the child wouldn't receive from his mother which he would have if he were to live in the company of his mother. A child-mother interaction unwittingly transfers to child the hidden cultural traits of mother. He is imbued with the values, norms and traditionally held folkways. When this interaction is lacking, the child would be deprived of these blessings.

Majority of the respondents are taking care of their children themselves during illness. As it is analyzed that 35% respondents are not present there during their (children's) illness, and they feel distracted and a sense of guilt not to be present there that time.

A child's illness is often accompanied with psychological upsetting. It is natural (and as the researcher made the observation) that the sick child would wish that his parents and more particular his mother would be with him. Children often suffer from fever and fever disturbs the mental balance of the child, making him fearful. He gets a feeling of fear from everything around him and naturally wants some one to rely upon under such circumstances. And who would he wish to be there other than his mother. But a working mother didn't get the time for it.

To overcome this difficulty, it has been suggested that the working women should take leave from the office and attend to their sick children. This proposition has inherent limitations.

Mothers are not entitled to unlimited leaves. Moreover, because of workload and commitment at office don't always make it feasible to take leave from the office.

Majority of the mothers were not satisfied with the performance of their mother roles. On the ultimate analysis 76% respondents confessed that they were not satisfied with the time they spend with their children.

The above findings lead the researcher to conclude that the working mothers are not satisfied with the performance of their mother roles. They are aware of the fact that their children are not getting their (mothers) proper attention. Due to lack of time they are unable to attend to their children.

Majority of the respondents feel that their children develop many problems because of their (mothers') absence. The main problem developed by such children is health problem – the health of such children deteriorates because of their mothers' absence. Some children suffer from nutritional and some from behavioural problems.

The analysis revealed that the mothers' presence is necessary for a child's physical as well as mental development and in her absence these problems are inevitable.

II: Problems of children of working women from the Age-Group of 4 to 12 years

Majority i.e. 80.5% of the respondents were being given lessons by private tutors and other agencies only 19.5% respondents were not receiving any private lessons (they were reading in the lower classes).

This goes to show that majority of the children of working mothers were getting additional guidance, which would certainly have positive effects on their educational performance. Families with working women are economically well off and as such can afford better opportunities for their wards.

Majority of the working mothers were not able to attend the school functions of their children. There are only 10.5% mothers who attend the school function of their children.

The above findings lead the researcher to conclude that the children miss their mothers in the school functions and are bound to suffer from the psychological problems and develop inferiority complex vis-à-vis other children.

The above findings lead the researcher to conclude that the children miss their mothers in the school functions and are bound to suffer from the psychological problems and develop inferiority complex vis-à-vis other children.

Majority of the respondents 95.5% did not or sometimes find their mothers at home after returning from the schools and only 4.5% found their mothers at home after returning from the schools.

This leads the researcher to conclude that the children need their mothers desperately when they return from the schools.

Majority of the respondents i.e. 65.5% respondents were fed up by other agencies and a substantial proportion of the respondents i.e. 34.5% were eat the food on their own during the absence of their mothers.

Majority of the respondents i.e. 65% felt the absence of their mothers during feeding time.

From the above findings it can be concluded that the children of working mothers are not satisfied on account of not being fed by their mothers. Most of the children didn't express it because of their love for their mothers but when the researcher looked into their eyes, they revealed a different story. It appears that every child wishes that he/she should be fed by his/her mother.

Majority of the respondents (79%) were taken care of by their mothers and some times by their fathers during illness. Rest of the respondents was taken care of by others. (Servants, grand parents etc.)

Majority of the respondents' (55%) mothers didn't go to the office when they (children) fell ill. 36% went to the office and 09% were not certain in their responses.

All the respondents in the sample were wishing that their mothers were with them during their illness. The reasons for wishing that their mothers' should be around during illness are: 32.5% of the respondents were of the response that they felt secure in presence of their mothers. 14% get a feeling of loneliness in absence of their mothers. 50.5% responded that they (mothers) could understand their problems better than others and 3% simply wished that their mothers should be around them.

The above findings revealed that the children need their mothers during illness. But the working mothers can seldom afford to remain with their children during illness. Many women have strict work schedule; they may not get time to spend a considerable length of their time with their children, and thereby causing irreparable damages to the psyche of their children.

Majority of the respondents of the sample (71.5%) were taken care of others during the absence of their mothers.

Rest (28.5%) was taken care of themselves. (They were grown ups).

Majority of the respondents i.e. 86.7% like the person who takes care of them during the absence of their mothers.

The conclusions drawn from the above findings indicate that children of working mothers are satisfied with the care takers. The children are tender hearted they like all those who show them any type of sympathy. They are without any bias. The researcher realised this fact during the research.

Majority of the respondents' mothers (66%) attends the household chores after returning from the office.

Majority of the respondents i.e. 77.5% said that their mothers attend the household chores on the holidays.

The findings revealed that most of the mothers in the sample are not attending the children after returning from the office and also on holidays. The children are already suffering from the "mothers' absence" during the day, but when they return back they attend household chores. They are unable to give their children a feeling of nearness which is necessary for their socialization.

Majority of the respondents' mothers (81%) were exhausted after returning from the office and are not in a position to attend their children.

It may be concluded, from the above findings, that the respondents, though of tender age, understood the problems of their mothers. They are not negative in their approaches. They do feel that their mothers undergo work over-load. They want to spend time with them but because of many roles they can't spend more time with them (children).

Majority of the respondents' (84%) said that their mothers stay outside homes for major part of the day. It is but natural that when the mother stays outside the home for around eight hours, she has not enough time to spend with her child. As shown in the above findings working mothers, after returning from the work, have to attend domestic duties. It shows that they have very little time to attend to their children; under such circumstances they can't guide them properly.

Majority of the respondents' mothers (75%) go on outings with their children. The results are positive. Mothers should somehow convey to her child the message of love and taking them on outings is the one way of communicating this message.

36.5% respondents would feel happy if their mothers gave up their jobs. 47% wouldn't feel happy and 16.5% were indifferent in their approaches.

The researcher feels that children of the sample were not proper in their approaches. Some of them said "No" but the researcher felt that they couldn't decide on what to say.

Majority of the respondents i.e. 87% responded that their mothers advised them to behave with others properly

From the above findings it may be concluded that the children are socialized by their mothers.

The researcher felt that the children had something else to reveal but they were diffident. The researcher also observed that the children had gloomy faces when they were asked something about their mothers.

Anyway the study of the working mothers reveals that mothers can't give their full attention to their children.

This is the ultimate reality. The absence of mother----child relation might have large repercussion on the development – physical, mental and psychological – of the child.

Even a cursory look at the above data gives a good idea about the impact of the working women on their children.

The work of women certainly does impact their children. The impact is not on a particular aspect of their lives but is multi-dimensional. The two most detrimental facts which make it difficult for working women to pay due attention to their children are lack of time and this reality is also borne out by the fact that 96% of women don't have sufficient time to spend with their children. Even on holidays and after work the majority of the mothers are unable to give company to their children. Just a meager portion of children, 8% and 2.5%, enjoyed the company of their mothers on holidays and after office work respectively. Even when the children are ill, majority of the working mothers are unable to nurse them. On this front the responses of the children was unanimous: that they want their mothers with them when they fell ill. Perhaps children need emotional support when they are ill, which can't be substituted.

It can be concluded that time is a great constrain on the working women. This lack of attention is certain to cause psychological/physical problems. Mothers' company is also indispensable for the proper socialization of the child. So it could be concluded that children whose mothers remain away from them for long periods wouldn't be properly socialized. Further work on macro level is needed to be conducted for realizing the actual nature of the social, psychological and emotional problems caused to the children. On account of the micro level scope of the present study, these things couldn't be ascertained. It would require holistic approach encompassing psychological and neurotic studies.

The researcher also came to the conclusion that the children of the working women are not fed properly. Even most of those mothers who breast-fed their children are not satisfied with the feeding of their children. The health of these children is bound to deteriorate. But on the face of it, such a trend was not observed. The reason might be subject to proper and balanced diet and that the working women get their children medically checked up on small instances. The same facility may not be available to the children of the non-working mothers.

However, these are not insurmountable problems. By proper guidance and expert applications of good methods, these problems could be solved.

The corresponding infrastructure needs to be developed to the level compatible with culture of working women. This would involve establishment of crèches, day care centers etc. as already mentioned elsewhere. The people of Kashmir are averse to keeping servants at homes, making the working women more irksome.

Governmental efforts are also needed. Legislation needs to be made in this direction. Working women should be made entitled to more leaves/holidays (with safeguards, that they might not misuse the provision). Working women should not be posted at far off places.

It is also concluded that children of these mothers have got used to the working of their mothers. They can't think of living under conditions contrary to it. Majority of the respondents' are not in favour of their mothers' giving up their jobs. They want to maintain the status quo. Our civilization has reached a stage where it is not possible to look back. Women have come out to work, we can't push them back. We have to change the environment and make it compatible with women's outside work.

Therefore, the things need to be re-adjusted. When a woman takes the plunge, she should realize that the traditional ways wouldn't work; she has got to change her life style and adapt to the new challenges and shed the shackles which keep her bound to the hearth. A woman, however, is not an isolated entity but is the infinitesimal part of a larger whole. A change in the womenfolk alone wouldn't suffice – the society as a whole has to bend to accommodate her transformed role. For to preserve the complex structure of the society, its each and every part must get re-aligned, otherwise it would buckle under the unbalanced strain and give way to chaos.

BIBLIOGRAPHY

Aggarwal, J.C. and Aggarwal, S.P., *Women's Education in India*, Concept Publishing House, New Delhi.

Aggreggar, C.E., *Graduate Women at Work*, British Federation University of London, 1966.

Anant, Suchitra, Rao, S.V.C., and Kapur, K., *Women at Work*, Sage Publications, New Delhi, 1986.

Arputhamurthy, Savitri, *Women, Work and Discrimination*, Discovery Publishing House, New Delhi, 1944.

Ashrafi, Ara Talat, *Muslim Women in Changing Perspective*, Commonwealth Publishers, New Delhi, 1992.

Baig, T.A., *Indian Women Power*, S. Chand and Company, New Delhi, 1978.

Banerjee, Nirmala, *Indian Women in a Changing Industrial Scenario*, Sage Publications, New Delhi, 1991.

Banton, Michael, *Roles an Introduction to the Study of Social Relations*, Tailstock Publications, London, 1969.

Bazaz, Prem Nath, *Inside Kashmir*, Gulshan Publishers, Srinagar, 2002.

Bhasin, K., *The Position of Women in India*, Shakuntla Publishing House, Bombay, 1972.

Biddle, J. and Edwin, J.T., *Role Theory: Concepts and Research*, John Willy and Sons, New York, 1966.

Blumberg, R.L. and Dwarki, L., *India's Educated Women Options and Constraints*, Hindustan Publishing House, New Delhi, 1980.

Bowels, Gloria, *Theories of Women's Studies,* Klein Rena to Duelli Rutledge and Kegan Paul London and New York, 1983.

Chakraborty, K., *The Conflicting Worlds of Working Mothers,* Calcutta Publishers Press, 1995.

Chakrapani, C. and Kumar, Vijay, S., *Changing Status and Role of Women in Indian Society,* M.D. Publications Pvt. Ltd., New Delhi, 1994.

Chandra, Jai Shree, *Women and Child,* Rawat Publications, New Delhi, 1993.

Chandra, Susmita, *Women and Economic Development,* B.R. Publishers, Delhi, 2001.

Chapman, Jane Roberts, *Economic Independence of Women: The Foundation for Equal Rights,* Vol. 1, Sage Publications, New Delhi, 1976.

Chauhan, Indira, *The Dilemma of Working Women Hostlers,* B.R. Publishers, New Delhi, 1983.

Chitkara, M.G., *Women and Social Transformation,* Ashish Publishing House, New Delhi, 2001.

Chodorow, N., *The Reproduction of Mothering,* University of California Press, Berkeley, 1978.

Chris, Janis, *The Sociology of Childhood,* Bastford Academics and Education Ltd., 1982.

Dabla, B.A., *Working Women in Kashmir,* Rawat Publications, New Delhi, 1983.

Dahl Storm, E., *The Changing Roles of Men and Women,* London Gerland Duckworth, 1967.

Dak, T.M, *Women and Work in Indian Society,* Discovery Publishing House, Delhi, 1988.

Davendra, Kiran, *Status and Position of Women in India,* Vikas Publishing House, Delhi, 1990.

Davis, Delia, *Women's Work,* Oxford University Press, 1976.

De Souza, A., *Women in Contemporary India,* Manohar Publishers Distributors, New Delhi, 1975.

Desai, N., *Women in Modern India,* Vora and Co. Publishers, Bombay, 1957.

Desai, Neera, *Women in Modern India,* Vora and Company, Bombay, 1977.

Dube, Leela, *Women and Kinship,* Vistar Publications, New Delhi, 1997.

Ellman, Mary, *Women in Between Female: Role in Male World,* Seminar Academics Press, London, 1972.

Epstein, C.F., *Women's Place,* University of California Press, Berkeley, 1972.

Everett, Jana Matson, *Women and Social Change in India,* Heritage Publications, Delhi, 1978.

Franzer, H.T., *Female Power in Changing India: An International Perspective,* Annu Prakashan, 1978.

Gadgil, D.R., *Women in the Working Force in India,* Asia Publishing House, New Delhi, 1960.

Ganjoo, S.K., *Kashmir: History and Politics,* Commonwealth Publishers, Delhi, 1998.

Garson, Kathleen, *Choices: How Women Decide About Work, Career and Motherhood,* University of California Press, Berkeley, 1985.

Ghosh, S.K., *Women in a Changing Society,* Ashish Publishing House, New Delhi, 1984.

Goode, W.H., *The Family,* Prentice Hall of India Pvt. Ltd., New Delhi, 1965.

Gothoskar, Sutata, *Struggle of Women at Work,* Vikas Publishing House, New Delhi, 1992.

Gupta, Sunit, *Role of Women in the Twenty First Century,* Anmol Publications, New Delhi, 1996.

Harper Bell, *Child Effects on Adults,* Lawrence Erlbaum Associates Publishers, 2977.

Hate, C.A., *Changing Status of Women,* Allied Publishers Pvt. Ltd., Bombay, 1986.

Jackson, *Role*, University Press, Cambridge, 1972.

Jayapalan, N., *Women Studies*, Atlantic Publishers, New Delhi, 2000.

Jewa, Sanjay Ketan, *Working Women and Modernization*, Ashish Publications, New Delhi, 1993.

Joshi, D.M., *Problems of Working Women*, Chetna Publishers, Delhi, 1961.

Kalbagh, C., *Social and Economic Dimensions of Women's Development*, Discovery Publishing House, New Delhi, 1992.

Kapor, P., *Changing Status of Working Women in India*, Vikas Publishing House, New Delhi, 1987.

Kapor, Promila, *Marriage and Working Women in India*, Vikas Publishing House, Delhi, 1970.

Kappurswamy, B., *Social Change in India*, Vikas Publishing House, New Delhi, 1972.

Kapur, M.N., *Social and Economic History of Jammu and Kashmir*, Jay Kay Book House, Delhi, 1992.

Kapur, M.N., *The History and Culture of Kashmir*, Jay Kay Book House, Delhi, 1992.

Kapur, P., *Marriage and the Working Women in India*, Vikas Publishing House, New Delhi, 1988.

Komarusky, M., *Women on the Modern World*, Little Brown Company, Boston, 1963.

Kumar, R., *Child Development in India*, Ashish Publishing House, New Delhi, 1988.

Kuzma, K., *Working Mothers*, Start Ford Press, Los Angels, 1980.

Lawrence, Walter R., *The Valley of Kashmir*, Chinar Publishing House, Srinagar, 1998.

Mac. Fadden Bernarr, *Womanhood and Marriage*, K.P. Publishers, Delhi, 1993.

Madhikar, Manoj, *Professional Housekeeping*, Rajat Publications, Delhi, New 2001.

Margolis, Maxine, *Mothers and Such*, University of California Press, 1984.

Mathur, Deepa, *Women, Family and Work,* California Press, Berkeley, 1992.

Mc. Candles, Boyd R., *Children and Youth,* Evans D. Ellis Dryden Press, 1996.

Menon, Indu M., *Status of Muslim Women in India,* Uppal Publishing House, New Delhi, 1981.

Mishra, A.D., *Problems and Prospects of Working Women in Urban India,* Mittal Publishing House, Delhi, 1994.

Mukta, Mittal & Gupta, Sunit, *Status of Women and Children in India,* Anmol Publications Pvt. Ltd., New Delhi, 1995.

Myrdal, A. Klein, *Women's Two Roles,* Rutledge, London, 1968.

Nye, Ivan F., *Family Relationships and Delinquent Behaviour,* John Willy, New York, 1958.

Pandit, S.K., *Women in Society,* Rajat Publications, New Delhi, 1998.

Parashar, Archana, *Women and Family Law Reform in India,* Sage Publications, New Delhi, 1992.

Ramu, G.N., *Women, Work and Marriage in Urban India,* Sage Publications, New Delhi, 1989.

Rani, Kala, *Role Conflict in Working Women,* Chetna Publishers, New Delhi, 1976.

Rao, Usha N.J., *Women in a Developing Society,* Ashish Publishing House, New Delhi, 1983.

Rao, V.K. and Khursheed, *Early Childhood, Care and Education,* Ul-Islam, S. Common Publishers, New Delhi, 1997.

Rapport, Rhone and Rapport, *Working Couples,* N. Robert, Rutledge and Kegan Paul Ltd., London, 1976.

Reddy, C. Raghunadha, *Changing Status of Educated Working Women—A Case Study,* B.R. Publishers, New Delhi, 1986.

Roy, Kalpana, *Women and Child Development,* Commonwealth Publishers, New Delhi, 2001.

Sahai, S.N., *Women in Changing Society,* Mittal Publishers, Delhi, 1985.

Sarkar, Chandana, *Juvenile Delinquency,* Daya Publishing House, Delhi, 1987.

Seeman, M., *Women Workers of India,* Asian Publishers, Bombay, 1966.

Sethi, R.M., *Modernization of Indian Working Women,* Vikas Publishing House, New Delhi, 1976.

Sethi, Raj Mohan, *Women in Developing Societies,* National Publishers, New Delhi, 1976.

Shafi, Aneesa, *Working Women in Kashmir,* Ashish Publishing House, New Delhi, 2001.

Shanthi, K., *Empowerment of Women,* Anmol Publications Pvt. Ltd., New Delhi, 1998.

Sharan, Raka, *Indian Women Workers,* Cosmo Publications, Delhi, 1985.

Sharma, B.R., *The Indian Industrial Workers,* Vikas Publishing House, New Delhi, 1973.

Sharma, Usha and Sharma, B.M., *Women and Professions,* Commonwealth Publishers, New Delhi, 1995.

Sharma, Usha, *History of Jammu, Kashmir and Ladakh,* Radha Publications, New Delhi, 2001.

Sinha, Pushpa, *Role Conflict Among Working Women,* Janaki Prakashan, New Delhi, 1987.

Sircar, Basobi, *Working Mothers and Adolescent Well-being,* Commonwealth Publishers, New Delhi, 1994.

Smart, C. Russel and Smart, S. Mollie, *Readings in Child Development,* Light and Life Publishers, New Delhi, 1972.

Smith, Peter, K. and Comie, Helens, *Understanding Children's Development,* Basil Black Well Ltd., New York, 1988.

Spock, Dr. Benjamin, *Baby and Child-care,* Rothenberg, Dr. Michael B. Simon and Schuster, Great Britain Ltd., 1992.

Srinivas, M.N., *Social Change in Modern India,* Allied Publishers, Bombay, 1966.

Srinivas, M.N., *The Changing Position of Women in India,* London Press, 1977.

Sullert, E., *Women, Society and Change,* World University Press, London, 1971.

Swarna Latha, E.V., *Woman's Education and Occupational Aspirations,* Discovery Publishing House, New Delhi, 1993.

Thomas, P., *Indian Women Throughout Ages,* Asia Publishers, Bombay, 1964.

Usharao, N.J., *Women in a Developing Society,* Ashish Publishing House, New Delhi, 1985.

Voydanoff, Patricia, *Women and Family Life,* Sage Publications California, 1978.

Wate, C.A., *Changing Status of Women,* Allied Publications, Bombay, 1963.

William, G., *Women and Society,* Nicholson and Walson, London, 1945.

Journals and Articles:

Aber, M.E. & R. Bernreuter, "Readings in Psychology of Parent-Child Relationship", *Journal of Genetic Psychology,* 1977.

Akhtar, S.S., "Attitude Towards Working Women", *Indian Journal of Social Work,* 1969.

Belsky and Hoffman, "Effects of Early Parental Employment on Children", a study conducted at Elizabeth Harvey University of Connecticut, 1999.

Brow, R.K., "The Employment of Married Women and Supervisory Role", *British Journal of Industrial Relations.*

Kontos, S.J., "Child Care Quality, Family Background, and Children's Development", *Early Childhood Research Quarterly,* 1991.

Luecken, Linda, "A Duke University Study on Stress in Working Moms", Veteran of the department of psychiatry at Duke University Medical Center in Durham.

Menaghan, E.G., "Parental Employment and & Parcel, T.L., "Family Life: Research in the 1980s." *Journal of Marriage and the Family,* 1990.

Ponce, Phil, "A Real Mother in the Modern World", A report on child care on brain development leads to a call for better child care, January 22, 1997.

Rouman, J., "School Children's Problems as Related to Presented Factors", *Journal of Educational Research,* 1956.

Singh, K.P., "Career and Family—Women: Two Roles", *Indian Journal of Social Work,* 1972,

Smith, S.M., and A.J. Davis, "Employed Mothers and Family Day-care Substitute Caregivers: A Comparative Analysis of Infant Care" *Child Development,* 1984.

APPENDICES

Interview Schedule: I

BIOGRAPHY:

1. Age group:
2. Sex:
3. Nature of the family:
4. Mothers' occupation:
5. Name:
6. Caste:
7. Who takes care of your child when you go for office?
   (a) Your in-laws. (b) Your parents.
   (c) Servant/Maid. (d) Take along to the place of work.
   (e) Any other.
8. Are you satisfied with this arrangement?
   (a) Yes. (b) No. (c) To some extent
9. If yes, why?
   (a) (Others) can do it properly
   (b) No other alternative
   (c) (Others) can understand them
   (d) Any other reason

10. If no, why?
    (a) (Others) don't understand his needs properly
    (b) (Others) are not interested in them.
    (c) Any other reason
11. When do you leave for office?
    (a) 8 A.M. (b) 9 A.M (c) 10 A.M.
12. When do you start preparing for the going to office?
    (a) 7 A.M. (b) 8 A.M. (c) 9 A.M.
13. Do you get sufficient time to attend to your child?
    (a) Yes. (b) No. (c) Indifferent.
14. If no, why?
    (a) Stay outside home for major part of the day.
    (b) After returning back from the work has to attend the domestic duties.
    (c) After returning back from the work is not in a position to attend children.
    (d) Sufficient time is not available.
    (e) Any other reason.
15. Are you satisfied with the time you spend with your child?
    (a) Yes. (b) No. (c) To some extent.
16. Do you feed your child before leaving for work or entrust the work to any other family member/ servant?
    (a) Yes, feed him/her myself.
    (b) No, entrust the work to someone else.
17. Do you feel that you feed him/her properly?
    (a) Yes. (b) No. (c) Indifferent.

18. Are you satisfied with the feeding of your children or you overfeed or underfeed him?

    (a) Yes. (b) No. (c) Indifferent.

19. Do you feel that such an arrangement tells upon the health of the child?

    (a) Yes. (b) No. (c) To some extent.

20. Do you feel that such an arrangement tells upon the psyche of the child?

    (a) Yes. (b) No. (c) To some extent.

21. Do you breast feed your child?

    (a) Yes. (b) No. (c) Indifferent.

22. If yes, are you able to feed him properly?

    (a) Yes. (b) No. (c) Indifferent.

23. If no, why?

    (a) Stay outside home for major part of the day.

    (b) After returning back from the work has to attend the domestic duties.

    (c) Don't have time.

    (d) Any other reason.

24. Do you think that your child needs you during the day?

    (a) Yes. (b) No. (c) Indifferent.

25. If yes, why?

    (a) Can feed the child properly.

    (b) Can look after the child in a better way.

    (c) Others can not take care of a child as properly as a mother can.

    (d) Children need mothers always.

26. When you return from work are you in a position to attend to your child?

    (a) Yes. (b) No. (c) Sometimes.

27. If no, why?

    (a) Because of fatigue.

    (b) Have to carry out domestic duties.

    (c) Sufficient time is not available.

    (d) Any other reason.

28. Who takes care of your child when he falls ill?

    (a) Yourself (b) Your in-laws.

    (c) Your parents (d) Relatives or friends.

    (e) servant/Maid.

29. Are you satisfied with the performance of your mother role?

    (a) Yes. (b) No. (c) To some extent.

30. Do you think that your absence during the day has created any problems in your child?

    (a) Yes. (b) No. (c) To some extent.

31. If yes, what type of problems?

    (a) Heath. (b) Nutritional

    (c) Behavioural (d) Any other

Interview Schedule: II

BIOGRAPHY:

1. Age Group:
2. Type of school:
3. Mother's occupation:
4. Nature of the family:
5. Sex:
6. Name:
7. Caste:
8. Who prepares you for school?

   (a) Mother (b) Father

   (c) Grand parents (d) Servant/maid.

   (e) Any other. (f) Prepare on your own.
9. Who teaches you at home?

   (a) Mother (b) Father

   (c) Grand parents (d) Tutor

   (e) Any other (f) No one
10. When any function is celebrated in your school (e.g. parents' day) does your mother attend it?

    (a) Yes (b) No

    (c) Sometimes.
11. If no, how do you feel?.

    (a) You get a feeling of loneliness and desperation.

    (b) You feel inferiority complex

    (c) You miss her

    (d) It does not matter to you.
12. When you return from the school, do you find your mother at home?

(a) Yes (b) No (c) Sometimes.

13. If yes, do you feel:
    (a) Happy (b) Secure
    (c) Care free (d) It makes no difference.
14. If no, do you....
    (a) Miss your mother
    (b) Do not miss her
    (c) Do not care about her
    (d) Wish that she were at home
15. What is your activity on holidays?
    (a) Study at home.
    (b) Study as well as play.
    (c) Go outside and play.
    (d) Watch T.V. and study.
    (e) Spend time with your parents
    (f) watch T.V.

Diet Habits:

16. Who feeds you during the absence of your mother?
    (a) Grand parents (b) Servant/Maid
    (c) Elderly siblings (d) Eat the food on your own
17. Do the servant/other family member feed you properly?
    (a) Yes (b) No
    (c) Indifferent.
18. If yes, does he/she feed you as good as your mother?
    (a) Yes (b) No
    (c) I feel the absence of my mother.

Health:

19. When you fall ill, who takes care of you?
    (a) Mother (b) Father
    (c) Grand parents. (d) Servant/ maid
    (e) Baby sitter at home or at day care centre.
    (f) Both mother and father.
20. Does your mother go to the office when you fall ill?
    (a) Yes (b) No
    (c) Indifferent
21. During illness, do you wish that your mother were with you?
    (a) Yes (b) No
    (c) Indifferent.
22. If yes, what is the reason?
    (a) You'd feel secure in presence of your mother.
    (b) You get a feeling of loneliness in absence of your mother.
    (c) You feel that if your mother were around she'd understand your problem better than others.
    (d) You just want your mother around.

Child care during mothers' working hours:

23. Who takes care of you during the absence of your mother?
    (a) Grand parents.
    (b) Elder and grown-up siblings.
    (c) Servant /maid at home
    (d) Baby sitter at the day care centre.
    (e) No one.

24. What are your feelings about the person who looks after you?
    (a) Do not like him/her (b) Like him/her.
    (c) Hate him/her (d) Like him/her more than your mother.
25. What does your mother do, when she return from her office?
    (a) Spends time with you.
    (b) Attends to house-holds chores.
    (c) Watches T.V.
    (d) Take rest.
    (e) Spends time with you and do the household chores.
26. When your mother returns from office, do you find she is:
    (a) Exhausted (b) Happy
    (c) Bad tempered (d) Upset
27. How long does your mother stay outside the home?
    (a) Four – Six hours
    (b) Six - Eight hours.
    (c) More than eight hours.
28. What does your mother do on holidays?
    (a) Spends time with you
    (b) Goes outside home.
    (c) Attends to house-hold chores.
    (d) Takes care of you and attends house hold chores.
29. Does your mother go for outings with you?
    (a) Yes (b) No
    (c) Sometimes.

30. Would you feel happy if your mother gives up her job?
    (a) Yes (b) No
    (c) Indifferent.

Socialization:

31. When you do any mistake or misbehave, what does your mother do?
    (a) Gives advice to you
    (b) Shouts at you
    (c) Beats you
    (d) Stops the pocket money she gives you.
    (e) Advises you how to behave with others.
    (f) Kisses and hugs you
32. Who teaches you, how to behave with elders?
    (a) Father
    (b) Mother
    (c) Grand parents
    (d) Elder and grown-up siblings.
    (e) Servant/maid at home
    (f) Both mother and father.

INDEX

A

Abbott-Shim, M. 33
Aber, M.E. 33, 111
Abnormal Psychology 33
Aggarwal, J.C. 105
Aggarwal, S.P. 105
Aggreggar, C.E. 105
Akhtar, S.S. 111
Anant, Suchitra 105
Arputhamurthy, Savitri 105
Ashrafi, Ara Talat 105
Automatic process 87

B

Baig, T.A. 105
Banerjee, Nirmala 105
Banton, Michael 105
Bazaz, Prem Nath 106
Behaviouristic approach 8
Behaviourists 8
Bhasin, K. 105
Biddle, J. 105
Biological woman 11
Blumberg, R.L. 105
Bowels, Gloria 105
Brow, R.K. 112
Bureaucratic jobs 18

C

Chakraborthy, Krishna 32, 106
Chakrapani, C. 106
Chandra, Jai Shree 106
Chandra, Susmita 106
Chapman, Jane Roberts 106
Chauhan, Indira 106
Chemical substances 75
Child care 44
    Development 1, 6, 12, 29, 33, 112
    Growth 19
Chitkara, M.G. 106
Chodorow, N. 106
Chris, Janis 106
Coleman, J.C. 19, 33
Contemporary society 3
Cultural roles 11
    traditions 11

D

Dabla, B.A. 106
Dahl Storm, E. 106
Dak, T.M. 106
Data Collection 42
Davendra, Kiran 107
Davis, Delia 106
Day care arrangement 47
De Souza, A. 107
Desai, N. 106
Desai, Neera 106
Developmental process 7
Diet Habits 74
Dube, Leela 107

E

Educational Guidance 69
    qualifications 21
Ellman, Mary 107
Emotional development 46
    issues 1
    psychology 11
    stability 36
Epstein, C.F. 107
Everett, Jana Matson 107

F

Familial influence 10
Family environment 10, 13
    organization 18
Feminist movement 3
Financial burdens 2
Frank Wood, E. 19
Franzer, H.T. 107
Fritz Pearls 8
Functional expectations 77

G

Gadgil, D.R. 107
Gainful employment 2, 4
Ganjoo, S.K. 107
Garson, Kathleen 107
Geson, Kathleen 107
Ghosh, S.K. 107
Goode, W.H. 107
Gorden Allport 8
Gothoskar, Sutata 107
Governmental organizations 18
Gupta, Sunit 107, 109

H

Harlow, Harry 33
Harper Bell 108
Harvey, Elizabeth 33
Hate, C.A. 107
Human activities 66
Humanistic Thought 8
Hurlock, E.B. 19, 20

I

Industrial Revolution 3
    world 91
Inferiority complex 71

Interpersonal Model 10
Investigation aims 36

J

Jayapalan, N. 108
Jewa, Sanjay Ketan 108
Johnson, M. Harry 19
Joshi. D.M. 108

K

Kalbagh, C. 108
Kappurswamy, B. 108
Kapur, M.N. 108
Kapur, P. 108
Kapur, Promila 32
Kashmir valley 37
Komarusky, M. 108
Kontos, S. J. 20, 112
Krishna Chakraborthy 22
Kumar, R. 108
Kuzma, K. 108

L

Lawrence, Walter R. 108
Liberation movement 3
Luecken, Linda 20

M

Mac. Fadden, Bernarr 109
Madhikar, Manoj 109
Maladaptive behaviour 8
Margolis, Maxine 109
Marital life 22
    status 5
Married women 1, 2
Maslow, Abraham 8
Mathur, Deepa 109
Mc. Candles, Boyd R. 109
Menaghan, E.G. 19, 112
Menon, Indu M. 109
Mental energy 82
Methodology 92, 93
Modern education 3
Modernized tradition 4
Motivational reasons 5
Mukta, Mittal 109
Myrdal, A. Klein 108

N

Non-working mothers 103
Nye, Ivan F. 109

O

Occupational mobility 3
Outside work 104

P

Pandit, S.K. 109
Parashar, Archana 109
Parental influence 7
Personality development 10
Physical fitness 77
Ponce, Phil 20, 112
Problems in Data Collection 42